SCANDALOUS GRACE

Grace, infusing and affecting all
aspects of our life journey

JONIE SCRUGGS

© Copyright 2022, Jonie Scruggs

All rights reserved. No part of this book may be reproduced, or transmitted in any form or by any means, electronic or mechanical, including photocopying and recording, or by any information storage and retrieval system, except in the case of brief quotations for use in articles, reviews, without written permission from the author.

The views expressed in this book are the author's and do not necessarily reflect those of the publisher.

WORLD WIDE PUBLISHING GROUP

7710-T Cherry Park Dr, Ste 224
Houston, TX 77095
http://WorldwidePublishingGroup.com
(713) 766-4271

ISBN: 978-1-0880-1234-5

CONTENTS

Foreword v

Chapter 1: Position Produces Practice 1

Chapter 2: Work It Out 12

Chapter 3: We Are Family 22

Chapter 4: Unity Is Not Uniformity 33

Chapter 5: Grace Changes Everything 45

Chapter 6: Still Standing 58

FOREWORD

Jonie Scruggs has been a disciple of Christ and a pastor of the Gospel for many years. I've known Jonie since he became engaged to my best friend's daughter thirty-plus years ago. I've had the privilege—though from afar—to see his testimony to the Lord Jesus Christ played out, and it's been a testimony I'm proud of. More importantly, it is a testimony of faithfulness that must bring a smile to the face of God our Father.

I love the writings of Paul, and especially the book of Ephesians. I believe the church in Ephesus held a special place in the heart of Paul, who spent three years there during his third missionary journey. While he was in prison in Rome, awaiting execution for his testimony and his unwillingness to refrain from preaching the Gospel, the church in Ephesus sent a visitor to Paul to encourage him. In response, Paul sent this letter back to the church, a reciprocal encouragement—from a man who was about to die.

In six short chapters Paul teaches us, in Jonie's words, "that grace gives us life, but then it carries us, keeps us, and continues to work on us." In other words, grace—God's *scandalous* grace—is the vehicle that moves us from conversion to the finish line, never leaving us to work our way alone on the path, but rather guided by God's precious Holy Spirit. This journey is not as much about what we do for Christ as it is about what God has done and is doing in us. As Jonie writes, the six chapters of Ephesians are "easily broken down into three and three... First, there is the Gospel story in the first three chapters. Second, there's the story of how the Gospel story affects my story in the last three chapters."

I pray that as you travel through the pages of this book, you will, as it says in Ephesians 3:18, "...have the power to understand ... how wide, how long, how high, and how deep" God's love is for us and for His Church, and the part you and I have to play in it.

Sharon K. Souza
Author of: "What We Don't Know"
and "Annie Walker"

CHAPTER 1

Position Produces Practice

Our position is not based on our practice. Our practice is based on our position, and our position is imputed by God.

You are invited on a journey with me. During this journey you will discover a life of mystery, empowerment, freedom, discovery, and adventure. Maybe you always imagined a life lived following Jesus was safe and uneventful. Perhaps you thought the Bible was old, outdated, and perhaps even worthless in your day-to-day life. Well, stay with me through these pages and you will discover excitement, relatability, and value for your life as we dive headfirst into a life lived in scandalous grace.

Second Peter 3:15-16 says, "And remember, our Lord's patience gives people time to be saved. This is what our beloved brother Paul also wrote to you with the wisdom God gave him—speaking of these things in all his letters. Some of his comments are hard to understand, and those who are ignorant and unstable have twisted his letters to mean something quite different, just as they do with other parts of scripture. And this will result in their destruction."

Did you catch the third sentence? "Some of his comments are hard to understand, and those who are ignorant and unstable have twisted his letters to mean something quite different…" Oh, make no mistake, this problem is nothing new! People misquoted and misinterpreted Paul long before the creation of social media. Peter called them "ignorant and unstable." Wow, Peter, tell us what you really think! I guess there was no politically correct agenda in those days. We still see this happening in both church and mainstream culture today, people twisting scripture and using it to mean something the original writers never meant. Has anyone ever twisted your words into something you never intended? Not cool.

Peter continues in chapter 3 verses 17-18, "You already know these things, dear friends. So be on guard; then you will not be carried away by the errors of these wicked people and lose your own secure footing. Rather, you must *grow in the grace* (emphasis mine) and knowledge of our Lord and Savior Jesus Christ. All glory to him, both now and forever. Amen."

"Grow in the grace." I emphasize growing in grace because this is key to your life journey. Most of us tend to think grit equals growth. Meaning, if you want to grow, you must have grit. You must grit it out, to live it out. We observe this philosophy across many areas of our lives. If we want to grow a company, we must get in, work it, grind it and grit it. We must work, push, pull, strive, and do whatever it takes. We must use all the correct principles of the business, or it will fail. If we want to grow our pecs, we must get into the gym and grit. We've got to grind it, push it and work it! Thus, we have a tendency, in our spiritual walk, to think grit equals growth. But what we see here in 2 Peter is not grit equals growth, but instead Grace = Growth.

As we walk this journey of spiritual growth together, we should approach this subject with an intense sense of awe. As I write these lines, I understand my ability to communicate this concept is limited. There's only so much I can say. I can communicate as eloquently as possible, but there is something supernatural about the Spirit of God, the Glory of God and growth by grace. There's something mysterious about grace. Therefore, God must do something we cannot do. We need Him to do what only He can do. God has to infuse His grace. There's something God must do today to transform your heart; to unlock your heart; to open your spirit and breathe life into you, as He alone can do. As a matter of fact, God said in the Book of Isaiah, "I will not share my glory with anyone else…" (Isa.42:8, NET). He refuses to share His glory! He refuses to share His brilliance with anybody. Spiritual growth is a very interesting process, right? What does it mean?

Second Peter is telling us, spiritual growth is more than a five-step formula. You're familiar with the fake formula, right? If we practice these five steps: Go to church, read our Bible, pray, tithe and serve, then we will grow in our relationship with God. However, I hope to reveal that spiritual growth is less about us and more about Him. Spiritual growth is God, through His grace, positions us to produce the right practices in us.

Grace Equals Growth

Peter provides a foundational principle when he says, "All glory to him, both now and forever!" (2 Pet. 3:18b). Meaning, our growth and relationship with the Father brings Him glory both now and forever, because our growth comes from Him. We don't get to piggyback on any of His glory. You may be wondering, "How do I know if I'm growing spiritually?" Perhaps a more suitable question would be, "Do I base my growth on what I do for God? Or do I base my growth on what God does in me?" These are valid questions. Let's explore them a little deeper.

Sometimes I receive video infomercials in my email. Perhaps you do too. I don't know why they send me this junk. Do they really think I will invest my hard-earned money to purchase their product because I watched a video? Wait, I suppose it does work sometimes. In any case, I watched a video introducing someone as a church "announcement specialist." Yes, you read correctly. The video was trying to sell an idea, sold by an "announcement specialist." Is this a real thing? Does this require a degree? Did I miss this course in college? Are announcement specialists necessary? Well, as I watched the video, the announcement specialist was standing in front of a congregation. Now, I don't know if there were people in the building. Maybe it was simply a simulation, you know, a virtual church. But I suppose that is irrelevant. He stood there on the platform and welcomed people: "Hey, welcome to, Announcement Church. We're so thankful you have taken your precious time out of your important and busy schedule to come here and worship with us." As I was watching the video I thought, *really?* Did I understand correctly? Is this what we are supposed to say? We're so thankful you've taken "your precious time" out of "your important and busy schedule" to come here and worship with us. All I could think was, he wants me to thank people for taking their precious time to come and worship the Creator of the universe. The One who spoke the universe into existence and created everything from nothing. The One who formed man with His hands and breathed life into him, making him a living soul. The God who sacrificed His one and only Son to come and die for His children. To forgive our sin and pour His grace on us, bringing us to life. Suddenly I started getting angry! How is it possible I'm being told to thank people for taking their precious time to worship the Designer and Creator of the universe; the One who grants and sustains life?

If we are growing in grace, wouldn't we desire nothing more than to approach His throne? Wouldn't we fall on our face in holy awe of His greatness? Wouldn't we set all our trivial pursuits aside for just one glimpse of His glory? The primary thrust of the video was to commend people for taking their precious time to come. I thought, "Wow, where is the glory of God in this?" I mean, I understand people have things to do. But we are designed to come together to worship God, to pour our hearts out to the Creator of the universe, the One who pours His grace on us.

As you can ascertain from this example, we often judge our growth based on what we do for Him. "God, I'm taking some of my precious time to go to a building and bless You with my presence. I'm going to bless You with my presence and I'm sacrificing my time to do so." Do we base our growth on what we do for Him, or do we base our growth on what He is doing in us?

When I think of all the good things God has done in me, I can't wait to worship Him! My time means nothing. My time belongs to Him. I will often say, "God, I worship You because I'm so thankful for all You have done in me. I don't deserve it, yet You pour Your grace on me anyway." Oh, come on, reader. When you think of all God has done in you, what is your time worth? He is worth everything. He is worthy of all praise. To be able to set aside an hour is minimal in the scope of all He has done in me; my heart yearns for Him. I don't feel I'm giving up anything. My heart yearns for His presence. I am in deep awe of my Creator. I long to worship Him. I am overwhelmed by His person. I don't worship because I owe a debt to God. I worship because I am overwhelmed with His glory, with His grace and with His presence. When I think of all He has done, not only for me but *in me*.

It's easy to thank God for what He has done for you. He gave you a house to live in. Perhaps you have a good job. You may not like your job, but it pays most of the bills. He's given you a respectable husband, maybe he sits on the couch a little bit too much, but he's still a good husband. He's given you a good wife. Maybe she—wait, I'll leave that alone. See what I mean, it's easy for us to thank Him for everything He's done for us. Oh, but when we think of all He has done *in* us, the softening of our hearts and the suppleness of our spirits, the spiritual life given by Him, all the other superficial stuff can pass by the wayside; all we need is what He has done and is doing in us.

Spoiler alert… Your position is not based on your practice. Your practice is based on your position, and your position is imputed by God. This ought to make you jump up and leap over a chair. Let me break it down. Colossians 2:9-10 says, "For in Christ lives all the fullness of God in a human body. So, you also are complete through your union with Christ, who is the head over every ruler and authority." That little word "So" links the thought that is to come, back to the previous phrase, "For in Christ lives all the fullness of God in a human body. *So* (or therefore) you also are complete through your union with Christ." You're perfect. Just like that. "You are complete through your union with Christ, who is the head over every ruler and authority." You are complete.

Our Position

We are complete in our position with Christ. We are perfect in Him. We are complete because our position is *imputed*—or given—to us. However, our practice is progressive. I'll say it another way: our *position* is immediate, but our *practice* is a process. In other words, you are the righteousness of God in Christ Jesus. Unfortunately, you don't always practice this perfectly. This is what Peter is communicating: you're not perfect because your *practice* is perfect; you're perfect because your *position* is perfect. It is by the grace of God you are in position. You are complete. You are perfect, lacking nothing. You have everything you need in Christ.

Do you see it? Our position is perfect, but our practice is imperfect. We are acutely aware of this, right? You're not complete because your practice is, you are complete because your position is. That's something to thank God for, because you're not the one who put yourself in position. You're not the one who decided yourself into a right position with God. You're not in a right position with God because you raised your hand, walked down an aisle or repeated some superstitious prayer. God was the One who placed you in the position of righteousness in Christ. It's a perfect position. Yet I know we say stuff like, "Well, I don't feel complete. I don't feel perfect."

We don't feel perfect because we sin. If you say, "I don't sin," you're sinning. Because we all do. We lie. We cheat. We steal items from our place of employment. We have terrible attitudes, don't we? Teenagers have bad attitudes sometimes, right? Hence, we don't always feel like we're perfect. Even in the good things we do, we often have wrong motives for why we do them. I am in no way advocating any of these sinful behaviors; I am simply showing we are not complete in our practice, but we are complete in our position because of Christ.

What I'm trying to say is, how you feel about your practice is a direct result of your practice, not your position. Sometimes you may feel discouraged because of your bad practices, but your position proves you are in the right place with God. So, sometimes you must tell your feelings, "Shut up!" Because we don't listen to feelings. We walk by faith, not by how we feel about what's going on. Now maybe the question you want to ask is, "How do I get my practice to match my position?" That's a great question! How do we align our practice with our position?

First, you can't produce the right practice in your own power. Your practice is produced through the power of God. 2 Peter 1:2-4 says, "May God give you more and more grace and peace as you grow in your knowledge of God and Jesus our Lord. By His divine power, God has given us everything we need for living a godly life. We have received all of this by coming to know him, the one who called us to himself by means of his marvelous glory and excellence. And because of his glory and excellence, he has given us great and precious promises. These are the promises that enable you to share his divine nature and escape the world's corruption caused by human desires."

Look at this phrase again: "May God give you more and more grace…" God gives you more and more grace and peace as you grow in your knowledge of God and Jesus your Lord. Here is the key: God, by His divine power, has given you everything you need to live a godly life. You receive this by coming to know Him. He has given you precious promises for His great glory. These promises enable you to share in His divine nature and escape the world's corruption. It is by His divine power you are in the right position, which means your position is not based on your practice. Your practice is based on your position, and your position is imputed by God.

His Divine Power

So, He places us in a perfect position by His divine power. But what about my practice? Here is how we often feel: Okay God, You saved me by grace, but now I need to earn my growth. I need to walk this out. I must get this done. I need to make this life work. I need to make this religious stuff work in my life.

Yet Peter said, "By his divine power…" So, God puts us in a position by His grace, then He walks with us to work out our walk, by His divine power. This is how He receives ALL the glory. You thought it was all about you! We are funny like that.

Suddenly, I get neither glory nor praise because I do something right. Suddenly, I understand it is by His divine power, not mine. This brings glory to God, not me. This thought connects us back to our very first verse, "All glory to him, both now and forever!" Forever means now, tomorrow, next week, next month, forever! Forever means at 8:37 a.m., and when you go to lunch, and when you lay your head down tonight. It means both now and forever. We are complete by His divine power. Yet everything in our culture and everything in our humanness kicks against this. Our thoughts contradict this because sometimes we think, "It doesn't feel as though I have the power; and it seems like my life is falling apart."

Maybe you're struggling in your marriage, or struggling with a relationship, or struggling with your teenagers, or struggling *as* a teenager because your hormones are raging. Maybe it feels like everything is about to explode! Perhaps you don't feel you have the completeness you need. You may even feel you have completely failed God.

Maybe you have said something like this: "If His divine power is in me, then why do I fail him? I told God I was going to stop losing my cool, but I lost it anyway. I promised not to watch porn anymore, but I have no power to quit. It doesn't seem like I can get my practice to align with my position. I say I'm going to forgive them, yet I struggle to forgive. I say, I'll never cheat again, and yet I fall back into repetitive behavior. I claim to trust God, but I have doubts, fears, worries, and concerns. I don't feel like I possess the power to live a godly practice." That was a mouthful, but trust me, we've all been there.

Listen, your feelings are a result of your practice. They are not the product of your position. God did not position you through *your* power; He positioned you through *His* divine power. Sometimes people tell me, "Well, I don't *feel* it." But the Father wants you to know, you are the righteousness of God in Christ Jesus. You are the head and not the tail. You are holy and you are pure. Not because your practice is perfect, but because your position is perfect.

Here is what I really want you to grasp. Ephesians 1:3-6 says, "All praise to God, the Father of our Lord Jesus Christ, who has blessed us with every spiritual blessing in the heavenly realms because we are united with Christ. Even before he made the world, God loved us and chose us in Christ to be holy and without fault in his eyes. God decided in advance to adopt us into his own family by bringing us to himself through Jesus Christ. This is what he wanted to do, and it gave him great pleasure. So, we praise God for the glorious grace he has poured out on us who belong to his dear Son."

Look at these verses again: "All praise to God, the Father of our Lord Jesus Christ, who has blessed us with every spiritual blessing in the heavenly realms because we are united with Christ." We have been blessed with *almost* every spiritual blessing. Right? That's not what the verse says, does it? It actually says, "*Every* spiritual blessing... Even before he made the world."

This blows my mind every time I read it. Before ever creating the world, God loved us and chose us. What? This is HUGE! Before He ever created the world, He loved you and chose you in Christ to be holy and without fault in His eyes. This is the perfect position, to be without fault in His eyes. Wait, what? That doesn't sound right; it's hard for us to grasp. It boggles the mind. God looks at us and sees us without fault. I wouldn't be able to look at you and think of you as being without fault. You wouldn't be able to look at me and think of me as being without fault. But when God looks at you, He sees you without fault. God determined in advance to adopt you and bring you into His family, by bringing you to Himself through Christ Jesus. He decided in advance. In advance of what? In advance of the world, in advance of *everything*.

His Great Pleasure

This is what He wanted to do, and it gave Him great pleasure. He brought us into position by His divine power for His great pleasure. This is such good news! We are His possession for His pleasure. So, we praise

God for His glorious, amazing, wonderful, strong, scandalous grace. He has poured His grace on those who belong to Him, to bring them into position with Him, bringing Him great pleasure. He does this work of grace in us because it brings Him great pleasure to do so. Think about this. Sometimes we feel God only puts up with us, almost as if He is barely enduring our presence. This couldn't be further from the truth. It brings Him great pleasure to pour His scandalous grace on us.

Can you say this with me today? "I am holy. I am pure. I am justified by Jesus' blood which has been decided and designated for me. Before the world was even created, He assigned His blood to me." Let this resonate in your heart and mind as you read this chapter. Your position is not based on your practice, because your practice is imperfect. Instead, your practice is based on your position, and your position is imputed or given by God.

We cannot practice our way into position with God, yet we try all the time. "I'm going to do better. I'm going to be nicer to my wife." And you should be nicer to your wife. I'm not saying you shouldn't. Don't even think about reading this, and then tell your wife, "I was reading a book and I learned I don't need to be nice to you anymore. So, cook me some food and clean up the table." Please don't say something so ridiculous! I'm not trying to get you cracked over the head with a rolling pin. So don't misrepresent my words to mean something they don't really mean, like Peter said people did to Paul. Don't even go there.

Yeah, we try to practice ourselves into position, but it never works. However, your position will always produce the right practice, every single time. When you get a glimpse of the grace and the goodness of God, when you are empowered by His divine power, He makes you capable to do what you should. Then, we walk out our practice through our position as we walk in His divine power.

Being part of a local church is important, but it's not what puts you in the right position. Reading your Bible is important, but reading doesn't practice you into position. Do you hear what I'm saying? Sometimes I think this is a scary topic for leaders or pastors to address, because it almost feels as though we're giving people a license to do nothing. However, this is a false feeling because when the grace of God is working in you, it will produce the right practice every single time. Grace will always work within you, what is necessary to work within you. Church attendance, prayer, Bible reading, tithing and service are all good practices, but they are not what makes you perfect. God placing you in the right position in Him makes you perfect.

Peter's final words were, "All glory to him, both now and forever!" Our spiritual growth gives God glory because our spiritual growth comes from Him. It is the work of grace in you that brings about the capacity to produce the right practices in your life. It's scandalous, I know. We will delve deeper in the chapters ahead. As we do, you're going to gain new glimpses into this scandalous grace that is greater than we ever imagined.

In the next chapter, we will see God working out what He has worked in us. When we feel trapped by life, circumstances, sin, a bad relationship or bad habits, God is always working it out. Put your seatbelt on, it's going to be a wild ride.

Let's pray...

Father, Your grace is all encompassing. Some of us say, "Well, you know I have a lot of struggles in my life, I don't always do what's right. I fail more than I don't. I feel like a failure and my spiritual walk doesn't seem to be working right." Lord, my prayer today is, flood us with Your scandalous grace, covering not only what we have done, but empowering us for what we will do, both now and forever. God, work Your scandalous grace in us. Strengthen and grow us today. We will bring You glory. Your glory will shine through our lives in the way we live and conduct ourselves. God, may Your glory shine even greater than we ever imagined it could. We pray this in the precious name of Jesus. A

CHAPTER 2

Work It Out

God's plan is more powerful than your prison.

At the end of the movie *Schindler's List*, Oskar Schindler (played by Liam Neeson) looks down at a ring given to him as a token of appreciation. With tears welling up in his eyes, he says, "I could have done more. I could have saved more. If I would have made more money, I could have saved more people. I didn't do enough." He steps towards his car, positioned to drive him away and says, "This car, why did I keep this car? Ten more people right there." As he turns away from his car in shame, he pulls a pin from the lapel of his suit coat. "This pin, two more people. It's gold, two people." The scene closes with him falling into a friend's arms as he weeps and cries aloud, "I didn't, I didn't, I didn't do enough!"

If you have ever seen the movie, it's a beautiful scene showing the passionate compassion of a man who poured his life out to save people from being slaughtered. Unfortunately for many, this scene represents a spiritual trap. The trap of never being able to do enough to please or earn their way into God's favor. Many spend their lives saying to themselves, "I can never do enough. I should sacrifice a little more. I should give more, serve more, pray more. I can't, I can't, I can't do enough!"

Culture puts a tremendous amount of pressure on people to perform. Work out and eat right to look right. Work hard to get ahead. Make something of yourself. Buy a bigger house. Get a nicer car. Date a hotter chic. Marry a better man. You've felt it right? Maybe you have even fallen into the spiritual trap of working to please God. Think about this trap for a moment. If it is necessary for you to work to merit God's favor, then it is necessary to work to retain God's favor. This could translate into more prayer, more worship, more reading, more church, more money, more time, more sacrifice, and the list goes on and on. But wait. If work is how we please God, when is it enough? How much is sufficient to secure His favor? How much must we pray, give, sacrifice, or do before He is pleased with us? It's a never ending, entangling trap!

God's Plan is a Good Plan

I have always had a bent towards the New Testament book of Ephesians. Perhaps you could say it's my "life book." Well, I just said that. Anyway, even though we explored some of Peter's writings in chapter one to lay the foundation of our position in Christ, Ephesians will be the launch pad and landing ramp for the rest of our journey through this book. As we journey together through these pages, my prayer is for you to experience the scandalous grace of God, which breaks the bondage of trying to perform to please God or gain His favor. I'm praying that God, through His grace, will transform and conform you into the man or woman He created you to be. He has a good plan for you!

Ephesians 1:3-8 says, "All praise to God, the Father of our Lord Jesus Christ, who has blessed us with every spiritual blessing in the heavenly realms because we are united with Christ. Even before he made the world, God loved us and chose us in Christ to be holy and without fault in his eyes. God decided in advance to adopt us into his own family by bringing us to himself through Jesus Christ. This is what he wanted to do, and it gave him great pleasure. So we praise God for the glorious grace he has poured out on us who belong to his dear Son. He is so rich in kindness and grace that he purchased our freedom with the blood of his Son and forgave our sins. He has showered his kindness on us, along with all wisdom and understanding."

Don't miss those four words in verse three, "*All praise to God...*" This is what grace does. This is the principal purpose of the book you hold in your hands. Grace, God's scandalous grace, always points praise to God. Grace glorifies and exalts God's glory. We don't get any props, no awards, no *attaboys* for the work of grace in us; it all belongs to Him. All of it. His grace is glorious, marvelous, wonderful, amazing, strong, extreme, and even scandalous! It reaches into the deepest pit to pull us out of the mud and mire. It sets our feet on solid ground and keeps us steady as we journey through life (see Psalm 40:2-3).

Ephesians 1:9-11 says, "God has now revealed to us his mysterious will regarding Christ—which is to fulfill his own good plan. And this is the plan: At the right time he will bring everything together under the authority of Christ—everything in heaven and on earth. Furthermore, because we are united with Christ, we have received an inheritance from God, for he chose us in advance, and he makes *everything work out according to his plan*" (emphasis mine).

God's plan is a good plan. It's not a haphazard plan, a happenstance plan, a maybe plan, a hopeful plan, or a backup plan. It is a good plan! Further, His will is to fulfill His good plan and He has the power to do so. This is good news for you. This is good news for me. We don't have to worry or wonder. We don't have to lay awake at night, losing sleep. We can rest in His wonderful, marvelous, scandalous grace, knowing His plan is good. His plan is to bring everything together under His authority, everything in heaven and on earth. Can you feel that? No matter how disjointed your life may seem right now, no matter what kind of mess you think you've made, God has a good plan to bring everything together. He doesn't stop there—there's more! Because we have been united in Christ, we have an inheritance. Can you imagine how cool this inheritance will be? It doesn't stop there; God chose you in advance to receive His inheritance and He always makes *everything work out according to His plan*. I've got great news for you: God is going to work it out!

God is Going to Work it Out

I can't reiterate this truth enough; He is going to work it out in your life. I have no idea what you're up against today. I can't imagine what you're going through. I'm not sure how much trouble you're in. I don't know how angry you are. I have no idea who hurt you or how much pain you feel in your heart. I don't know whether you're depressed, worried or afraid. But I'm here to give you good news. God is going to work it out. This is in His good plan. We all have our own problems. Okay, I'm going to rephrase that. You're probably living the perfect life, but I have problems! I don't like it when the people in front of me are driving too slowly. Sometimes I imagine crashing into the rear of their car with my truck. Yes, I confess, I have anger issues. But I have good news, too. God is going to work it out, for you and even for me. He will work it out according to His good plan.

Are you tracking with me? We need God to work it out because we're all a little crazy. You may profess to have your act together, but if I asked your friends or your spouse, trust me, they would have a long list of your issues! I'm just saying, we all have issues. It would be very easy for you to read *information* and not really experience *transformation*. Therefore, you need God to do within you what you can't do for yourself. This is why I need God to do within me what I cannot do for myself. God has a better plan for you than merely reading this information; He has life transformation. There is life changing, scandalous grace transformation when we are in His presence. I can't transform you or your situation. I can't work it out for you, but I know someone who can. I know a grace that can. I know a scandalous grace that can transform your life as well as the situation you find yourself in.

God's Plan is More Powerful than Your Prison

Most of Paul's writings were penned while he was in prison. You wouldn't have hired Paul if he had applied for employment in your company. You would have taken one look at his record and said, "Sorry, bro, we're not hiring today." What I'm saying is, Paul had a criminal record. Many of Paul's letters were composed while he was bound. You may think you can't accomplish anything great for God because you're in bondage; bondage of bitterness, unforgiveness, hate, anger, lust, greed, or you fill in the blank.

When Paul placed pen to paper, to write the church in Ephesus, he was in prison again. This is so ironic. Think about it. Paul wrote to people on the mysterious plan of God while in prison. Perhaps you weren't aware of this fact. Please hear me, you don't have to be behind bars to be in prison! Fear can be a prison. Depression is a prison. Anger and road rage is a prison. An inferiority complex is a prison. Anxiety is a prison. Do you hear what I'm saying? It is not necessary to be behind iron bars to be in prison. The enemy places people in prisons all the time, but I've got good news for you! God's plan is more powerful than your prison. That's the goodness of our God. His plan is more powerful.

God Uses Opposition to Produce Opportunity

The opposition you are trying to avoid could be the opportunity God uses to launch you forward into the purpose and plan He has for you. Are you getting this? God uses what you perceive as opposition to create opportunity. The opposition Paul experienced in prison gave him the opportunity to think and write. His opposition provided the opportunity to address the church in Ephesus. So, your prison could potentially be the platform God uses to project you into your purpose. Let me put it like this: Not only is God's plan more powerful than your prison, but like Paul, God's plan could produce *because* of your prison.

His plan will produce through the prison you find yourself in. Please lean into this concept. Compassion can be produced in prison. Many years ago, I suffered a traffic accident that injured my back. At the time I was only 17 years old, so I thought everything would be fine. I mean, at 17, I was invincible, wasn't I? Well, turns out I wasn't. I was in so much pain I was losing the use of my legs. After living in pain for years, I had my first back surgery at 26, then my second back surgery at 36. I eventually underwent a total of three operations on my back. I spent years in excruciating back pain producing compassion for people who have back pain. I've been in back pain prison, so I have great compassion for people in a prison of back pain. Can you see it? Your opposition today might be what God is using to bring the compassion you need for someone tomorrow.

Nothing Goes to Waste in God's Plan

Nothing goes to waste in God's good plan. Remember, Paul wrote about God's mysterious plan during his time in prison. Paul's imprisonment was not wasted because he spent his time writing about God's plan. Listen to me, God is going to work it out. No matter what prison you find yourself in, God has a good plan, and He will work it out. Not because of who you are, but because of Whose you are. Not because of how good you are, but because of how great He is. This is His scandalous grace.

Paul had previously visited Ephesus. Then God gave him a heart for Ephesus, and while he was there, many heard the Gospel. Many believed in Jesus. You can read this amazing missional journey in Acts 19. While Paul was in Ephesus, God gave him an incredible outpouring of grace. Paul had the ability to perform mind boggling miracles. Once, a handkerchief touched the skin of Paul, and when it touched someone else, they were healed! Yes, you read that correctly. The handkerchief touched the sick and they were healed. This is insane, right? Sounds like a televangelist gimmick. I can hear it now, "Send $100 and receive a blessed cloth. Lay it on your sick grandmother's forehead and she'll be HEEEAAWLLD-A!" That's televangelist, for healed.

OK, let's get to the real story. There were seven brothers who came up with the brilliant idea of imitating Paul's power. They decided if Paul could perform miracles, so could they. In the book of Acts, those seven brothers were referred to as the sons of Sceva. An interesting note to consider is, Sceva, their father, was a religious leader. He was a priest (I'll come back to this later). The seven brothers decided to cast out demons by saying, "I command you in the name of Jesus, whom Paul preaches, to come out!" Well, the demons were not impressed, at all! The evil spirit replied, "I know Jesus, and I know Paul, but who are you?" I wonder if the demons used a little stronger language. Perhaps words were omitted from the Bible for parental guidance purposes. Well, the man with the evil spirit jumped on them, overpowered them, and attacked them with such violence they ran away, naked and bleeding. Reminds me of some scenes from the old movie, *The Exorcist*.

You Can't Live Under the Covering of Someone's Grace; God Has Grace for You

Listen to me, here's what I'm saying. You can't walk under the covering of someone else's grace. Not your father the priest, and not Paul the Apostle. God has grace just for you. That's right, just for you. You cannot walk under the covering of Mom and Dad's grace, because God has grace for you. God stepped down through time and space to pay the price on the cross for your grace. Listen church goer, you can't worship under the covering of someone else's grace. Oh, I know that doesn't make you shout, but I'm telling you, you can't worship under the covering of somebody else's grace. God has grace for you, just for you. Teenager, your parents' relationship with God isn't a free pass for you. God has grace for you! Men and ladies, you cannot walk under the covering of someone else's grace. Husband, the relationship between your wife and God does not cover you by osmosis or association. Wives, your husband's relationship with God doesn't cover you. You cannot walk under the covering of someone else's grace, because the enemy will run you out naked and bleeding. God has grace just for you. That's good news.

Well, as you can imagine, people in Ephesus started talking about what happened to Sceva's seven sons. As a result, a holy fear spread throughout the city, and the name of Jesus was honored, and people's lives were transformed. Many people became believers and confessed their sinful practices. Those who had been practicing sorcery brought their incantation books and burned them at a public bonfire. The value of the books was several million dollars. That's right, several million! Now that's a big bonfire. As you can imagine, the message about Jesus spread like a wild bonfire (pun intended) and had a powerful effect on people's lives.

However, there were some people who didn't want this bonfire faith to spread. Trouble began to stir through a man named Demetrius, a silversmith who had a large business and employed many craftsmen who manufactured silver shrines of the Greek goddess Artemis. Demetrius called his employees together, along with other employees in similar trades, and addressed them as follows in Acts 19:25b-27: "Gentlemen, you know that our wealth comes from this business. But as you have seen and heard, this man Paul has persuaded many people that handmade gods aren't really gods at all. And he's done this not only here in Ephesus but throughout the entire province! Of course, I'm not just talking about the loss of public respect for our business. I'm also concerned that the temple of the great goddess Artemis will lose its influence and that Artemis—this magnificent goddess worshiped throughout the province of Asia and all around the world—will be robbed of her great prestige!"

The Enemy Works Against You Because God Works In and Through You

That event provoked outrage among those who earned their living in the trade. Soon the whole city of Ephesus was filled with confusion. Everyone rushed to the local amphitheater. People were shouting, some one thing and some another. Everything was in chaotic confusion. In fact, most of them didn't have a clue as to why they were there. Does this ring a bell for you? People get so stirred up about politics, religion, racism, social justice, or any number of hot topics. They insult each other through social media and lose sight of what really matters.

Demetrius stirred up trouble for Paul because God was using Paul. The enemy will always try to stir up trouble when people are walking in the good plan God has for them. If you're wondering why the enemy is working so hard against you, it could be because God is working so hard in and through you. When we do that which God has called us to do, the enemy always lifts his head against us.

God's Plan is More Powerful Than Your Prison

Ephesians 1:2 says, "May God our Father and the Lord Jesus Christ *give you grace and peace*" (emphasis mine). Not confusion, disorder, frustration, worry, anger, anxiety, or fear, but may He give you grace and peace. Paul wrote this while he was in an Ephesian prison. It's interesting the words he used in chapter 1, verse 11, "Furthermore, because we are united with Christ, we have received an inheritance from God, for he chose us in advance, and he makes everything work out according to His plan." Think about that for a second. Paul states God makes everything work out according to His plan, while Paul is in prison! Paul, who was in prison for preaching the Gospel, could have easily said, "This didn't work out very well for me."

Perhaps you find yourself in a prison of frustration or anger. Maybe you jump from relationship to relationship. Perhaps you're worried about life, teenagers, finances, college or the future. When you find yourself in prison, it would be easy to say, "God's word says everything works out according to God's plan, but this doesn't seem to be working for me." Yet Paul, while in prison, says God works everything out according to His plan.

Our exasperation is often connected to a prison of expectation. We tend to believe God should work out our situations to our specifications. Sometimes we pray ourselves into a prison. "God, this is what I'm dealing with, and this is how I want you to work it out. I've thought this through so this is what I need You to do!" Oh, don't act all "holier than thou" like you've never prayed this kind of prayer. No one walks around with halos over their head all the time. Those words have escaped my lips on occasions, so I'm fairly certain you have prayed something similar. However, God's ways are higher than our ways. His thoughts are higher than our thoughts. He has a better plan than we could ever think or imagine. He truly has our best in mind. He is working all things together for the good of those who love God and are called according to His purpose.

I wonder, what do you need God to work out in your life today? Because His plan is good. You must hear what I'm saying. His plan is always good. Ephesians 1:9 says, "God has now revealed to us his mysterious will regarding Christ—which is to fulfill His own good plan." God's good plan is more powerful than your prison.

God's plan is more powerful than your depression. His plan is more powerful than your fear of what might happen tomorrow. God's plan is more powerful than your prison, and God could be using your prison today to produce the compassion you need to help free somebody from their prison tomorrow. Case in point, if Paul had been so busy going from place to place, preaching crusade to crusade, from city to city, he may not have had the opportunity to write the remarkable book of Ephesians we read today.

In the following chapter, we will journey into God's good plan to bring together His beautiful, diverse, multicultural family. He is going to work it out according to His good plan. His plan was to bring different peoples together into His big, beautiful family. So, let's journey a little deeper into His scandalous grace.

Let's pray...

Father, I pray today You would seal a work in the hearts of teenagers, moms, dads, grandparents or anyone reading this book. Seal the assurance that You are working out everything according to Your plan. Lord, we pray and ask it. We step into and lean into Your perfect plan. In Jesus' name. Amen.

CHAPTER 3

We Are Family

We are part of the greatest family because it's the family born in the heart of God.

Family is either a joyous topic or a thorn buried deep under your big toenail. Seldom are there many emotions in-between. You have probably heard friends make statements like, "Well, they are family and family is hard!" On the other side, people may say, "Family is everything. I would do anything for my family!" I don't know which side you're on today. But I know this, God has a mysterious and glorious plan for His family and His plan is better than any we could possibly imagine.

Ephesians 2:14-19 says, "For Christ himself has brought peace to us. He united Jews and Gentiles into one people when, in his own body on the cross, he broke down the wall of hostility that separated us. He did this by ending the system of law with its commandments and regulations. He made peace between Jews and Gentiles by creating in himself one new people from the two groups. Together as one body, Christ reconciled both groups to God by means of his death on the cross, and our hostility toward each other was put to death. He brought this Good News of peace to you Gentiles who were far away from him, and peace to the Jews who were near. Now all of us can come to the Father through the same Holy Spirit because of what Christ has done for us. So now you Gentiles are no longer strangers and foreigners. You are citizens along with all of God's holy people. You are members of God's family."

Sister Sledge sang a song in the late 1970s titled "We Are Family."

> Everyone can see we're together, as we walk on by
> (Fly) and we fly just like birds of a feather, I won't tell no lie
> (All) all the people around us, they say, can they be that close
> Just let me state for the record, we're giving love in a family dose
> We are family, I got all my sisters with me
> We are family, Get up everybody and sing

This song wasn't exactly my musical style. I was more of a metalhead. You know what I mean, a headbanger. However, it was a very influential song back in the day. Look closely at these lyrics, "We are family. I've got all my sisters with me. We're family. So, get up everybody and sing." Then the verse went, "Everyone can see we're together as they walk on by. And we fly like birds of a feather, I won't tell no lie. All the people around us, they say, can they be that close? Just let me state for the record, we're giving love in a family dose."

Sounds great, right? This kind of family sounds awesome. This kind of family should excite you. However, families don't always look like this. It sounds good on the surface. It's like, "Wow! I would love to be part of a family like that." Herein lies the problem: Many of us don't experience this kind of a family. We don't often see this family model in our culture. Even in the church world, we talk about the family of God and being part of His family. However, if we relate the family of God to the way many family trees look, family can be very dysfunctional.

Family can seem like a bunch of angry cats trapped in a box. Can't you imagine the cats in a fighting frenzy? I had bad experiences with cats, so forgive me if I'm not a cat fan. Anyway, back to family. Often, the family feels like crazy cats. It feels like dysfunction. There's absenteeism in families and families who are uninvolved with one another. Honestly, a lot of families are completely broken, fighting, gossiping, slandering, and pitting members against one another. Oh, you thought I was referring to your family? I was talking about many local church families! Yet, Jesus, through the Apostle Paul stated, "For Christ himself has brought peace to us. He united Jews and Gentiles into one people when, in his own body on the cross, he broke down the wall of hostility that separated us." Yet, we still experience separation in our homes and churches. So, what's going on?

I remember a specific situation with a young family who had gone through divorce. Both parties were using their children as pawns to punish their former spouse, withholding information, badmouthing the other spouse in the presence of the children. The children would have to listen to each parent spew poison about their other parent. Poisoning the children with hatred, bitterness and resentment is a terrible way to treat the children you say you love. Word to divorced parents: Either forgive and move on with your life or keep your poison to yourself!

There's also abuse, infidelity and slandering. So, sometimes when we read verses like this where God is talking about a beautiful, peaceful family, we ask, "Wow, where can I find this kind of family?"

Every Brick in the Wall Has Been Broken Down

Look at Ephesians 2:14 again. It reads, "For Christ himself has brought peace to us." We could all use more peace in our lives. "He united Jews and Gentiles into one people…" God took two peoples and turned them into one. "When, in His own body on the cross, He broke down the walls of hostility that separated us." What is Paul saying here? What is he trying to communicate when he mentions breaking down the walls of hostility that separated us? Every brick in the wall has been broken down. The walls we have constructed between us, and others have been broken down. Every wounded heart is broken down. Every pain of abuse is broken down. Every dysfunction in our lives is broken down. Christ, on the cross, broke down every brick in the wall of separation. Not even Pink Floyd can build a wall able to stand.

What Paul was dealing with in Ephesus was a wall of separation between Jews and Gentiles. The Jews had learned over 600 laws from the Torah. The Jews had rules and regulations the Gentiles were not aware of and really did not understand. This separated the Jews and the Gentiles because the Jews felt superior while the Gentiles felt inferior because they did not comprehend all that God required in The Law.

Now, It's Us Together

Paul is exhibiting, through Christ's finished work, there is no more Jew and Gentile. You may be wondering how this is of interest to you. This signifies to us, there is no more "us and them." There is no more "you and me." Now it's us together. Indeed, Christ Himself has brought us peace. He has brought together two peoples and broken down the walls of hostility. There is no more separation.

This was the mysterious plan of God before He breathed life into mankind. This was His plan all along. Ephesians 3:6 says, "And this is God's plan: Both Gentiles and Jews who believe the Good News share equally in the riches inherited by God's children. Both are part of the same body, and both enjoy the promise of blessings because they belong to Christ Jesus."

Look at this again: "*Both are part of the same body*, and both *enjoy* the promise of blessings because they belong to Christ Jesus." Both, not just one. No separation. No segregation. Not "us and them." We are both part of the same body. This is something to celebrate. This should be shouted from the highest mountain. "We are no longer separated; we are part of the same body!"

Did you know you are to enjoy the promise of God's blessing? That's right, I said, "enjoy." Let's look at the word *enjoy*. Sometimes we are so engrossed in our own mess and failures, we have difficulty enjoying anything. But you are to enjoy the promise of God's blessings. He desires life for you and life more abundantly. You can walk in the joy, peace, faithfulness, and goodness of God. David, a man after God's own heart, said in Psalm 27:13, "Yet I am confident I will see the Lord's goodness while I am here in the land of the living." That is good news for us all!

Unification Overcame Separation

God brought blessing by bringing together two peoples. The two of them became us together. God did this by ending the system of law with its commands and regulations. He broke down the wall separating "us and them," and brought the two together. He made peace between Jews and Gentiles. In case you think I'm only talking about the Ephesian church, He brought peace between the churched and unchurched peoples. He brought peace between religious and non-religious people. He brought peace between blacks and whites, reds, and yellows. He brought peace between Baptist, Pentecostal, Lutheran, and "LutherBaptiCostals." He has brought peace to all. He brought us together, and we are family.

Christ reconciled both groups to God by means of His death on the cross. The hostility between them was killed. Unification overcame separation. Oh, you should shout a little bit. God brought about unification which conquered the separation. He broke down the walls and united people who were divided.

I'm going to be honest with you. Some questions that struck me while I was writing this were, "Really? We don't have anymore walls? Are we unified? There is no more separation?" Because it seems to me, we live with walls: racial walls, ethical walls, socioeconomic walls, doctrinal walls, religious walls, moral walls, political walls, musical style walls and the list goes on. People spew rhetoric like, "I don't go to church with them because we are too different. I need to find people like me. I only need to be with *my* people." But Paul was trying to show us that your people are their people, and their people are your people. We are family.

I have heard very prominent pastors who spend much of their time teaching about the differences between one another. They will tear down one group, while calling out another group. So, I ask you: "Where is the unification? Where is the unification overcoming separation?" I don't believe highlighting differences is the heart of God. God's heart is to break down the walls of separation.

You are my brother or sister. I love you the way you are. I'll walk with you when you stumble. I'll walk with you when you fall. I'll help pick you up. I'll walk with you through the trials, tribulations, and hardships of life. I'll walk with you because we are family. There's no walls between us. This is the heart of God! He reconciled two into one, so there's no more "us and them," there's only us together.

We are in this together. God destroyed the hostility between one another. No longer should we reject someone because they don't look like us. No more should I have contempt for a person who doesn't speak like me, dress like me, believe like me, worship like me, or vote like me. God overcame separation with unification. We are family.

Young and old, black, and white, rich, and poor, happy, or sad, reunite. We come together, the churched and the unchurched; every denomination can lay aside differences and say, "We may not agree on everything, but we can agree on this: We will love you and walk with you. We will spend time with you. We can worship together because we are family."

Ephesians 2:17 says, "He brought this Good News of peace to you Gentiles who were far away from him, and peace to the Jews who were near. *Now all of us* (emphasis mine) can come to the Father through the same Holy Spirit because of what Christ has done for us." Did Paul say, "Now, all of us…?" Wait, this can't be right. Not all. Surely, he didn't literally mean all of us. Paul probably meant all of us, except for people who vote differently from me, all of us except for those who don't worship as I do. No, as a matter of fact, I'm pretty sure Paul was talking about all of us. All of us can come to the Father through the same Holy Spirit because of what Christ has done for us.

This is scandalous grace! It's scandalous because it doesn't fit within a small-minded mentality. It's scandalous because God broke down the walls of separation. Nobody is better than anyone else. He broke down the walls and it's scandalous. It's scandalous when we were taught, "they are different from me, and I am different from them." But God wants you to know; when we come to Him in faith, we are all His people. We are all together. He made two into one and we are family. This is scandalous.

Stranger Danger Destroyed

"You Gentiles are no longer strangers and foreigners. You are citizens along with all of God's holy people. You are members of God's family." Here's what this means for us: stranger danger is destroyed. Grace put stranger danger to death and destroyed it. God often breaks something down to build something new. He will even put something to death to make something else come alive. He will destroy our ideas, our mentalities, our fears, our worries, and our anxieties. He will even destroy our dreams so He can direct our destiny.

Maybe you wanted to be married before you were twenty-five. But God knew if you married the wrong person, they would ruin your life. So, your dream had to die to direct you towards your true destiny. My dream was to be a rockstar. I wanted to be the next Jon Bon Jovi! I recognize that dream ages me, but I had a dream. God had to destroy my dream to direct my destiny. God must do that sometimes.

I use the phrase "stranger danger" on purpose, because many of us were taught as children that strangers were dangerous. Don't talk to strangers because they could hurt you or abduct you. Regrettably, the "stranger danger" concept crept into many local churches.

When I was a student pastor in Las Vegas, there were a plethora of different types of teens in our group of young people. Some were very churched teens, and some, well, not so much. Some of our students played in an underground screamo band and were going to be in concert at a nearby music scene. I decided to take some students to the concert so we could all hang out together and support the band. After all, these guys were fellow youth group friends, and it would be fun. I mean, what could go wrong?

We showed up at the club scene, one of those underground clubs in Las Vegas. Everything was going great. The teenagers were having fun, talking, joking, and really excited about seeing their friends in concert. As we walked towards the building, we realized we didn't know where the entrance was. We searched for a few minutes with no success. I think they design the music venues this way so not everyone can stroll in off the street. That's my guess anyway.

While looking for the entrance, I saw several teenagers hanging out by some cars in the parking lot. To be honest with you, they were kind of strange looking. It was back in the '90s, so they had multi-colored hair, Mohawks and spikes coming out of every piece of clothing they wore. This was pretty typical back then. They had chains hanging from different parts of their bodies and they were smoking something—I'm not sure exactly what. I mentioned to one of the "more conservative" students, "Hey, I'm going to ask those guys where the entrance is." After all, they looked like they had been here before, and probably knew their way around.

Makes sense, don't you think? When I headed in their direction, a couple of the teens who had come with us grabbed my arm and said, "Oh, Pastor, wait, they look dangerous. They might hurt you!" I tried to assure them this was not my first concert. I walked over to these very "dangerous" looking teenagers and said, "Hey, guys, where's the entrance? We're here to see some friends in concert but can't find our way in." I wasn't completely sure what to expect but figured I could handle a few teenagers if things went south. I never looked behind me, but I was pretty sure the teens I had brought were cowering down between a couple of the parked cars. One of the teenagers I addressed looked up from the thing he was fidgeting with in his hands and stated with a very friendly and polite voice, "Hey, man. Yeah, if you go right around this corner and down the alley, you'll see the entrance on the right." And just like that, *stranger danger* was dispelled.

Look again at Ephesians 2:19, "So now you Gentiles are no longer strangers and foreigners. You are citizens along with all of God's holy people. You are members of God's family." Through the work Christ did on the cross for those who belong to Him, stranger danger is destroyed!

We are members of God's beautiful family. God's mysterious plan has always been to unite this enormous multicultural, multi diverse, multiethnic family. It was His plan from the beginning. It was always

His design to bring together a family who loved one another, hung with one another, and supported one another. You may not think this sounds like the average local church. But this is still God's mysterious plan!

Social Media is Not God's Design for Family

Newsflash, this just in… social media is not God's design for the family. Don't get the wrong idea, social media has its place. But when all hell is breaking out in your life and you get the cancer report from the doctor, you're going to need more than a few prayer emojis in your comment section! Every time someone places a prayer emoji on someone's page, I'm not convinced they're praying. Let me put it this way. You are going to need people who love you, walk with you, pray with you, hold you, and spend time with you. This is what God designed the family to look like. This was His mystery plan before the foundation of the earth.

Think about it for a second. What would it look like if we were really part of a church family who loved each other? Who loved each other, no matter what. This may be difficult for you to imagine. Many people have never seen an example of that type of family. It is hard for many to comprehend what a true Father looks like, when fathers were absent, or parents were divorced. Maybe someone cheated on you in a relationship or you experienced infidelity in your marriage. Often, we have no context for what a loving, loyal, praying, and tolerant family looks like. Even so, what would happen if we decided to love each other unconditionally? No matter what somebody did, didn't do, said, or didn't say. What would life be like if we were part of a family, a family conceived by God, who loved one another without conditions. What would happen if we chose to love one another without stipulations? What would it be like to be part of a family who truly loved to see one another succeed? What could happen? Imagine if you experienced godly unity. What would it look like to have true unity in the church family?

Paul wrote to the church of Ephesus, but I believe it applies to the whole universal Church. What might happen if we became a family faithful to each other? What would life be like if, at the first sign of difficulty or disagreement, people didn't decide to walk away? What might happen if we decide, "I'll be faithful. I'll stand with you when we agree and when we don't. I will stay with you through the good and the bad, through the happy and the sad." How great would that be? How many people could be reached if we were a church like Paul describes, involved in one another's lives? What would be possible if we were a church family who fought for one another, our community, and our world. What would our world be like if we became the Church God designed us to be?

I'm not talking about the church building; I'm talking about the church family. God planned this kind of family long ago, and He adopted us who were far from Him into His family. We are part of the greatest family, because it's the family born in the heart of God.

Maybe you have a great family. I hope and pray you do. But even your great family fails in comparison to the family birthed in the heart of God. "All the people around us, they say, can they be that close? Let me state it just for the record, we're giving love in a family dose." In case you're offended because I quoted some lyrics from a '70s song, let me end this chapter with a Bible verse. "So now you Gentiles are no longer strangers and foreigners. You are citizens along with all of God's holy people. You are members of God's family."

This is not an easy concept for those who have no context of this kind of family. Some of us have no idea how to be a father because we didn't have a father. Some of us don't know how to be good husbands because we didn't see our dads being good husbands. We may not know how to be a woman or a man of faith because we didn't grow up in a household of faith. So, we find ourselves floundering through life, saying, "God, I don't know how to do this. I don't know how to live this. I don't know how to be this." Yet God still brought us together, those who were far and those who were near. He brought two together and made us one.

In the next chapter, we will journey into the world of unity, another foreign concept to our culture. However, I believe unity is key to being a godly family.

Let's pray...

God, information doesn't bring transformation. We ask the Holy Spirit to transform our lives so our hearts, mindsets and lifestyles reflect Your word. God, destroy our former mindsets and vain imaginations. Bring us into a new position with You, where walls are broken down, where unity overcomes separation, and we literally walk in unity with one another. We need you, God. We're praying, and we ask it, and we believe it in Jesus' name.

CHAPTER 4

Unity Is Not Uniformity

> **God calls us to unity, not uniformity.**

I grew up being taught that to have unity you must have uniformity. It may not have been stated in those exact words, but I basically learned that unity meant thinking like and believing like me. If you don't think or believe like me, we don't have unity. This mindset translated into "dress like me, look like me, worship like me and live like me." If you don't agree with every single point of Scripture exactly like me, we can't associate together. After all, bad character corrupts good company. Please don't misunderstand me, I had great parents and I grew up in a great heritage, but there was an unspoken rule, *unity equals uniformity*. Perhaps you have heard statements like this before, "They're probably not going to make it to heaven. If they're not part of us, they're probably not going to make it." I honestly don't believe that those who said things like that were trying to set themselves up as judge and jury. But the truth is, if we are not careful, we can mistake u-ni-ty for you-be-like-me.

Let's look at Ephesians 4:1-7. "Therefore I, a prisoner for serving the Lord, beg you to lead a life worthy of your calling, for you have been called by God. Always be humble and gentle. Be patient with each other, making allowance for each other's faults because of your love. Make every effort to keep yourselves united in the Spirit, binding yourselves together with peace. For there is one body and one Spirit, just as you have been called to one glorious hope for the future. There is one Lord, one faith, one baptism, one God and Father of all, who is over all, in all, and living through all. However,…"

Before we finish verse seven, let's do a quick English lesson. We're not back in high school sitting in our English class, but "however" is an interesting word for me. It is a word introducing a statement which seems to contradict what has already been said. Very quickly, let me give some examples. "However" works like this. "I really want to lose weight; however, I really like eating chocolate cake." How about this one? "I really want to work out and get into shape; however, I love sitting on the couch playing video games." Do you see how this works? "I want to get out of debt; however, Amazon calls my name in the middle of the night."

This is how "however" works. We don't always realize we're using the word; however, we utilize it often. See what I did there? "I really want to grow spiritually; however, I struggle to find time to invest in my spiritual walk." So, are you picking up on what I'm saying? I'm not attempting to call you out or embarrass you; I'm merely making the point that we use the word often. We may not actually verbalize the word, but we exhibit it with our actions. We want to change; however, actions speak louder than words. It's a contrast but can seem like a contradiction.

Unity Does Not Require Uniformity

So, Paul points to this truth in verse 4: "There is one body and one Spirit, just as you have been called to one glorious hope for the future. There is one Lord, one faith, one baptism, one God and Father of all, who is over all, in all, and living through all. *However* (emphasis mine), he has given each one of us a special gift through the generosity of Christ." Although Paul may seem to contradict himself, he's using contrast to make a point. Do you see it? There's one, one, one, one, one, one and one; however, each one has a special gift through the generosity of Christ.

Paul is communicating that unity is not uniformity. In other words, we may be united, but God has a special gift just for you.

I'm so thankful God planned a church of diversity. God had a mysterious plan through His scandalous grace to create a church with a diversity of gifts, personalities, and ethnicity; a church with different backgrounds and cultures coming together as Jews and Gentiles, blacks and whites, reds, and yellows, yes, even Republicans and Democrats. It's a church of diversity who can worship together, grow together, and serve people together, despite our differences. It's a church where you don't have to look like me, sound like me, talk like me, dress like me, or vote the same as me; but we can love and function in unity without the necessity of uniformity. Because unity is not the same as uniformity.

The Gospel Story and the Gospel Story Affecting Our Story

I love the book of Ephesians! It is such a beautiful book about God's mysterious plan. Ephesians is made up of two distinct sections. There are six chapters, easily broken down into three and three. But it also tells one story in two parts. First, there is the Gospel story in the first three chapters. Second, there's the story of how the Gospel story affects my story in the last three chapters. These two sections are linked together with one word. In the first half, Paul so eloquently speaks of how God brought us to spiritual life. Christ brought two groups of people together and created one out of two. Paul explains how God is building His mysterious, beautiful family of different cultures into one glorious Church. Then Paul links the two sections together with one word, "therefore."

You may have heard this before, "therefore is always there for a reason." See what I did there? It was a little play on words. "Therefore" always links what was previously said with what is stated next. First, it should be pointed out that the Bible was not written in chapters and verses. Hence, when Paul wrote to the church in Ephesus, he wasn't cleverly breaking this down into six chapters of three and three. He was merely writing to

Ephesus about God's mysterious plan. Later, all chapters and verses were added to provide quick references. Thus, about halfway through Paul's letter to the church in Ephesus, he links the Gospel story with the effect of the Gospel story using the word "therefore."

Look at verse one again. "Therefore I, a prisoner for serving the Lord, beg you to lead a life worthy of your calling, for you have been called by God." In other words, he's saying that the scandalous grace of God brought you to spiritual life, linking Jews and Gentiles together and made two peoples into one. Because God is building His church of multiple ethnic people, therefore, Paul, a prisoner for serving the Lord, begs you to lead a life reflecting this transformed life in Christ. WOW, what a mouthful! Paul links the Gospel story to the effect on our life story. Live a life worthy of your calling, for you have been called by God. If you are following Jesus, if you're living your life to glorify Him, if you have been brought from death to life, you are following Him because He has called you to do so.

Called by God

Do you hear the "scandalous grace" power of this statement? This is a powerful proclamation: God Himself has called you. As a matter of fact, Isaiah 43:1 tells us, "But now, O Jacob, listen to the Lord who created you. O Israel, the one who formed you says, 'Do not be afraid, for I have ransomed you. I have called you by name; you are mine.'" Did you catch the last part of this verse? God knows your name. That's right. Of all the millions of people in the world, of all the billions of people who have ever walked this planet or whoever will, God knows YOUR name! Watch this, He has called you by name. God says to you today, "I have called you by name; you are mine." Hear me today. You have been called by God. God has called your name.

God Calls Us Out to Call Us In

First, He called you out. Now, I don't mean in the sense that He called you out to embarrass you. He called you out of darkness. He called you out of death. He called you out of disobedience, rebellion, promiscuity, drunkenness, and impurity. He has called you out. When God calls you by name, He doesn't just say, "Hey, John, climb your way out." To be called by God literally means for God to reach down, pull you out and redeem you to rescue you out of your mess. He calls you OUT. But calling you out is not the conclusion. He calls us out to call us in.

Second, God doesn't merely call us out. He doesn't say, "Hey, I'm calling you, so you need to stop all the fun things you were doing. You can't do those anymore." This isn't the call at all. He calls you out to call you in. He calls you out of darkness into His marvelous light. Out of death, into life. Out of debauchery, into holiness. Out of promiscuity, into purity. He calls you into His strength, power, and presence. There used to be a saying, "You don't have to go home, but you can't stay here." That's not God. He not only calls you out. He calls you in.

Can I make a confession? I should come clean. Just because I have been called out of my mess, doesn't mean all my mess is out of me. I still have some mess in me. I have a temper and sometimes I lose my… cool. To be completely transparent, there are times I can fly into a rage! I almost wish my anger was directed towards big problems, but the truth is, it's usually trivial things that shouldn't even matter. I'm not proud of myself. On the contrary, I'm embarrassed when I behave this way. Now, before you get all self-righteous and judgmental, you have some mess in you too. Just because God has called you out of your mess, doesn't mean all your mess is out of you. Our mess may not look the same, but it's still messy!

Watch what Paul says in Ephesians 4:2, "Always be humble and gentle. Be patient with each other, making allowance for each other's faults because of your love." I believe Paul basically means, "Don't judge others based on your progress." Be humble. Don't fall into the trap of thinking because you've matured in an area, you have the right to look down your nose at someone because you don't think they have reached your spiritual maturity. How arrogant. Don't buy into the lie!

We rarely judge ourselves by someone who is further along in their faith journey. This wouldn't make us feel good. We tend to compare ourselves with someone whom we think isn't doing as good as we are. This trap makes us feel better about ourselves. So, Paul urges, "Always be humble and gentle. Be patient with each other…" Don't hate, that's what he's saying. Be patient and make allowances for each other's faults because of your love.

Now, I really wanted to find out exactly what "be patient" meant in the original translation. So, I studied by looking at the Greek, Hebrew, Spanish, and French translations. I researched this phrase in every translation I could find. I wanted to know exactly what Paul was referring to when he said, "be patient." I studied it hard because I thought, God, there must be something in this verse we're missing. Is there a language barrier? What does Paul mean when he says, "be patient?" You know what I found? When Paul said, "be patient," he intended for us to be patient with each other. Yes, it's quite simple. When Paul said, "Be patient and make allowance for each other's faults…" He was saying, be patient, don't look down your nose at people, placing yourself in a hierarchy so you feel superior to them because you have matured in an area of your life. Reading your Bible more often or memorizing more scripture doesn't make you superior.

Be patient with each other. This statement almost sounds comical in our culture, right? Patience? You must be kidding. No one has any patience with anyone. You say one thing wrong, and you are out of my life. Don't you dare post a political preference on social media because you'll get unfriended in a millisecond. You are cancelled! We're not patient with anyone. If you don't act like me, believe everything exactly like me, then we can't be friends. I feel like we're back in elementary school! "You're not my friend anymore. You're stupid. I don't like you anymore."

In the beginning days of planting The Journey Church, I once had a Sunday morning guest who vowed not to come back, saying, "I'm not coming back because the pastor wears skinny jeans." We're not patient with anyone. Sometime later, we had a young girl who was extremely offended by something one of our pastors said from the platform. She was so offended, she got up during the message, stormed out and explained to me later, "There is nothing you can say to change my mind, I am so offended, I'll never be back!" Now, to be fair, what the pastor said was out of line and I did have a conversation with him about his comment. The point is, this young lady was unwilling to be patient with the pastor or make any allowance for his faults, as it instructs in Ephesians 4:2.

It appears we don't want to have patience or make allowance for anyone's faults, except for our own, of course. If anyone says anything we don't like, we quickly cut them off from our lives. This is so sad because we are all flawed. Not one of us is perfect. We all make mistakes. We all say ignorant things. So be patient and make allowance for each other's faults.

News flash, I'm flawed. You may not know me personally, but you should know I have faults, shortcomings, and failures. Yes, I have faults, but this just in, so do you. Yes, I said it, you have faults. Your close friends have faults. Your church has faults. Stop jumping from relationship to relationship or church to church trying to find flawless people because you're never going to find what you're looking for. Even U2 still hasn't found what you're looking for. Besides, if you do, you'll ruin everything because, as you guessed, you have flaws. So stop jumping, stop running and stop quitting. Stop trying to find the perfect church or the perfect relationship because they don't exist. Stop and be patient. Be patient with each other. After all, we are family, and unity doesn't require uniformity! Stop flipping each other off, getting mad and walking out the door. Stop avoiding people you no longer associate with due to past conflict or offence. Be patient and make allowance for each other's faults.

Why? Because of your love. This word *love* is the word agape and means *love without contingency*. We do not understand love without contingency, because, in most cases, our love is based on what we feel. Our love has conditions. "I'll love you if you tell me what I want to hear.

I'll love you if you do what I want you to do. I'll love you if you act like I want you to act." Our love has contingencies and conditions. But Paul tells us to be patient because of our love, a love that says: "I'll be patient when you fail. I'll be patient when you succeed. I'll be patient when you talk to me. I'll be patient when you ignore me. I'll be patient when we agree. I'll be patient when we disagree. I'll be patient when you tell me what I hate to hear. I'll be patient when you tell me what I love to hear."

Be patient because of your love. I am so glad God is patient with me. I'm so glad He is patient with you. Second Peter 3:9 says, "The Lord isn't really being slow about his promises, as some people think. No, he is being patient..." He has been patient for your sake. He's being patient with you. When you were far from Him, when you were running, when you were angry, when you were rebellious, when you were struggling, when you were hurting, when you were bitter, and when you were depressed, He was being patient for you. When you were broken, when you were dead in your sin, He was being patient for you. He was being patient because He loves you, because He loves you no matter what. It's not conditional. He just says, "I love you and I'm going to be patient for you." He loves you through His glorious, scandalous grace. It's scandalous, I know. His love isn't contingent on what you did. It isn't conditional on what you're going to do. God has been and continues to be patient for you.

Keep Unity

Second Peter 3:3 says, "Make every effort to keep yourselves united in the Spirit, binding yourselves together with peace." Paul exhorts us to keep unity. But here is what's interesting. He says keep unity, but then he says, bind yourselves together. In other words, unity is not easy. Think of it this way. When we bind ourselves together in marriage, we must work together to make the marriage work. When we are bound together by working together, our reward is a fulfilling marriage rather than the wreck of divorce. Likewise, when we are bound together in God's Church, the reward is fulfilling relationships rather than the alternative ruined relationships. Paul paints a picture. Unity is not always easy, because it's not about uniformity. It's not about being the same. I'm not the same as my wife and she's not the same as me, but we are bound together in unity and the result is a beautiful relationship. I can't leave her. I don't want to leave her! I can't run away whenever I'm angry, and I don't want to. Why? Because we are what? We are bound together in unity.

Could it be, when we lack patience, we lack love? It's difficult to walk out on people when you are bound together in unity because of love. Ephesians 4:4-6 says, "For there is one body and one Spirit, just as you have been called to one glorious hope for the future. There is one Lord, one faith, one baptism, one God and Father of all, who is over all, in all, and living through all." That is a lot of unity. Count them: one, one, one, one, one, one, one. There are seven ones in his statement. Why did Paul use seven ones right here? Is it because there are seven days in a week? Is it because seven is the perfect number? Is it because it took Israel seven days to march around Jericho so the walls would fall? Hear me out, there's unity in seven. There is something about seven in connection with unity. Paul is saying there's one body, one Spirit, one glorious hope, one Lord, one faith, one baptism, one God and Father of all. One, one, one, one, one, one, one.

There is unity in seven. There is unity in the Church. There is unity in the body of Christ because we are bound together as one. We must not be easily offended and leave. We shouldn't divorce ourselves from our family. As true followers of Jesus, we should have no desire to do so! Because we are one. We are bound together in unity, but unity is not uniformity. The very next verse says, "However, he has given each one of us a special gift through the generosity of Christ." Did you see it? True unity doesn't require uniformity. True unity unleashes diversity.

True Unity Doesn't Require Uniformity; It Unleashes Diversity

My wife and I are in unity, but we are not even near uniformity. I am so much better looking than she is. No, I'm kidding. It's the exact opposite. I think we should move on here. We are in unity, but we are not the same. She sees details I don't see. She is a detail-oriented person; I am not. She knows that details are important, and I find them laborious, because we are not the same. When I ask her about her day, all I want are the facts. When she tells me about her day, she gives me the play-by-play in slow motion! Not what I was asking for. When I tell her about my day, it only takes about two to three sentences. To tell you the truth, sometimes I can capture my entire day in one sentence. This is a win for me. A great day and I didn't even waste time babbling about it. As you can see, we have unity, but not uniformity.

Paul addresses the church of Ephesus as two groups of people who God has united into one. One faith, one Lord, one baptism, one hope, etc., with everyone having different gifts because true unity unleashes diversity. Someone told me years ago, if you marry someone exactly like yourself, one of you is unnecessary. This is a good example of why God made a way for His people to be in unity with great diversity.

Diversity is free from controversy when unity overcomes uniformity

Unity gives you the power of diversity when diverse people come together and say something like, "We may not agree on everything, but we can agree on something. We will work together, worship together, serve God together and reach our community together. We will do this together because we are in unity." God gave each one of us a special gift. I'm so glad we don't all have to look the same, think the same or even believe the same. Diversity is free from controversy when unity overcomes uniformity.

Unity unleashes diversity because God has a special gift for each one of us. Let that sink in. God has given each one a special gift. God has given you a special gift, just for you. Gifts aren't about you being the elite. They're not so you can say, "My gift is better than your gift. Don't you wish you had my gift?" This is not what our gifts are for. Yet sometimes we do this. Sometimes we even look at each other's gifts and say, "Oh, I would like to have their gift. I wish I were like them. Oh, I wish I could preach like them. Oh, if I could lead worship like them. If only I had the entrepreneurial spirit of them." No, He has a gift, a special gift for you. You don't need anyone else's gift and they don't need yours. God has set something special within each of us.

Offense is an Event; Being Offended is a Choice

We are called by God. We're called out. We're called out of our mess into His grace. We're called out to be called in. We're called to be patient. This may sound harsh but stop getting butt-hurt over every little offensive thing someone does to you. Offense is an event; being offended is a choice! If you are offended by what I have just said, you are part of the problem rather than part of the solution. Be patient, make allowance for one another's faults, because we all have faults. Make allowance for different ideas, failures, mistakes, and faults. We are called to unity, not uniformity, because unity unleashes diversity.

Ephesians 4:11-12 says, "Now these are the gifts Christ gave to the church: the apostles, the prophets, the evangelists, and the pastors and teachers. Their responsibility is to equip God's people to do his work and build up the church, the body of Christ." God calls us to unity, not uniformity. Unity is part of God's plan to build up the Church. It's not for you to flaunt your gifts in somebody else's face. It's not for you to think more highly of yourself than you should. It's not for you to compare your gift to someone else's gift. Your gift helps build up the Church, the very Body of Christ.

In our next chapter, we will discover that grace changes everything. Not only our past, but our present and our future. Grace transforms our family relationships, work ethic, church family relationships, attitudes, hurts, pains, and the list is endless. Grace is more than forgiveness for our past, grace infuses and affects every aspect of our life journey.

Let's pray...

Father, You have called us to a life unshackled from uniformity. We are not called to look like, act like, dress like or vote like everyone else. We are called to live in unity with our brothers and sisters in Christ. Thank you for calling us out to call us in, into Your love, mercy, healing, peace, and into Your scandalous grace. Thank You for giving us the grace and power to live in unity, unleashing diversity. When we are overwhelmed by people's expectations of us, we can rest in Your peace. We're praying, asking, and believing in Jesus' name.

CHAPTER 5

Grace Changes Everything

> *Grace not only produces spiritual life;*
> *grace also produces a life lived by the Spirit.*

I was the founding/lead pastor of The Journey Church of Waller for about seven years. During those years I was privileged to witness God completely transform people's lives by His grace. I recall a young man whom I'll call Mitch. He and his family attended sporadically through our formative years. They would arrive late and leave early. Mitch was aloof, cynical, and sometimes argumentative. His wife was very withdrawn and seemed self-conscious around people. However, something changed around year two. They started truly engaging, interacting with people, volunteering, and building relationships. Eventually they relocated about 45 minutes from our location, and they tried to connect to a local body close to where they moved. However, they had become so connected to TJC they eventually began to make the lengthy drive to worship with our church every weekend and the same drive home. During their next five years with TJC, God turned this cynical, arrogant, even argumentative young husband and father into a loving, humble man of God. As he stepped up his leadership and became the man God had created him to be, his wife also flourished into a friendly, loving part of the family. Why? Because God's scandalous grace changes everything.

Another man, whom I'll call Billy, had been with TJC for about five to six years before grace really grabbed his heart. Billy came from a stricter religious background, so when he began to connect, he was very skeptical. It took about five years, but I can remember so many times Billy coming to me after our worship service and saying, "Wow, that was just what I needed to hear. What you said changed my whole perspective. Thank you." Once when I was preaching through Ephesians, Billy came to me afterwards and said, "I have loved that portion of scripture in Ephesians for a long time. But you brought so much clarity and a new perspective to this, that I will never be the same." Grace changes everything.

I'd love to tell you about a young woman whom I'll call Tina. She had been part of a traditional church for years. The funny thing is, she first visited TJC because she felt obligated after I spoke at a community event she oversaw. After a couple years, Tina told our entire church body, "After connecting with TJC, I have seen it modeled and really understand how to lovingly accept people. For years, I lived critical of people, but now I see how to accept people where they are, without self-righteous expectations of who I think they should be. I can love them right where they are." This is not something we accomplished as a church. This happened in her life because grace changes everything. God's grace is scandalous, and it changes everything.

I'll give you one more example, this time of a man whom I'll call Mark. When I met Mark, he was drunk. As a matter of fact, every time I saw Mark, he was drunk. Mark was an alcoholic. Often, he would come to my house around 8:00 a.m. on a Saturday and have coffee with me while he was drunk. We would talk about life, marriage, politics, the world, Jesus, work, and cartoons. After his first cup of coffee, he would pull a can of beer out of his jacket pocket and drink it. He always kept an extra beer on him, just in case he needed a pick-me-up. Mark really liked beer. One day, he phoned me while I was on my way home from the office. He was drunk when he called. He was always drunk. I heard him say to me, "Man, I don't know what the hell is goin' on. I'm a mean son-of-a-bitch, but for some reason I don't want to be like this anymore. Will you come read the book of Mark to me? My name is Mark, so I want to know what Mark in the Bible is talking about." Guess what? I went and read the book of Mark to him that day.

Full disclosure, Mark continued drinking too much. Me reading some Bible verses didn't magically turn his life around. One hot, Texas, August morning after his wife left for work, Mark was drunk. While outside on his wooded property he stumbled, fell, and knocked himself out, after locking himself out of his house and losing his keys. Sounds like a bad day, right? Well, his day got even worse. About 5:30 that evening, his wife was frantically knocking on my front door, screaming, "Help me, Mark can't walk! Help, I can't get Mark into the house! Help please, he needs help!" They lived across the street from me, so we both ran to their house and found him leaning against his truck, convulsing, and mumbling under his breath. I couldn't understand what he was saying, but I was pretty sure it wasn't good. He was in bad shape. He had been outside all day with no food, no water and most importantly, no alcohol. His wife and I worked desperately to carry Mark through the garage, into the house, while he mumbled and reached for random items. After finally getting Mark to their bedroom, I asked his wife to call 911. It took some persuasion, but she finally consented to check Mark into the emergency room.

After three months of detox and another several months of rehabilitation, Mark returned home. The very next Sunday he was worshiping with TJC and probably missed only a handful of worship services over the next four years. He was sober, serving, worshiping, learning, discipling, and giving. God had brought about a complete transformation of life in him! Personally, I had never seen such a drastic change of life. Grace changes everything.

A few months after returning from rehab, Mark woke one morning and found his wife dead in the hallway of their home, from alcohol poisoning. I walked Mark through the funeral arrangements and kept close by his side. To be honest, I wasn't sure how he would cope. Would he begin drinking again? Would he become angry at God? Would he question everything God had done in his life over the past year? No, absolutely not. Mark leaned on his church family. He remained open to what God was doing in him and on his behalf. He grieved, cried, processed, served, loved, stayed sober and healed. Why? Because grace makes us new, but it doesn't end there. Grace then carries us from where we are to where Jesus wants us to be. God's scandalous grace changes everything, every part of our life!

I could give you examples of Greg, Jim, Ernie, Joslin, Zan, and so many more scandalous grace stories about people from so many different backgrounds and experiences. The bottom line is those stories would all include the wonderful, glorious, amazing, scandalous grace of God. Why? Because grace changes everything!

Ephesians 4:11-12 says, "Now these are the gifts Christ gave to the church: the apostles, the prophets, the evangelists, and the pastors and teachers. Their responsibility is to equip God's people to do his work and build up the church, the body of Christ." Did you catch it? Jesus is still working on the Church, through His gifts to the Church, because He loves His Church!

Verses 13-16 continues, "This will continue until we all come to such unity *(not uniformity)* in our faith and knowledge of God's Son that we will be mature in the Lord, measuring up to the full and complete standard of Christ. Then we will no longer be immature like children. We won't be tossed and blown about by every wind of new teaching. We will not be influenced when people try to trick us with lies so clever, they sound like the truth. Instead, we will speak the truth in love, growing in every way more and more like Christ, who is the head of his body, the church. He makes the whole body fit together perfectly. As each part does its own special work, it helps the other parts grow, so that the whole body is healthy and growing and full of love."

Grace changes everything. Not most things; everything. Not part of your life; every part of your life. Not your life only; everything about you. Grace changes everything about you from top to bottom, inside and out. His scandalous grace changes everything.

Ephesians 4:16 starts with this: "*He makes the whole body fit together perfectly* (emphasis mine). As each part does its own special work, it helps the other parts grow, so that the whole body is healthy and growing and full of love." Wait, who makes the whole body fit together perfectly? He, God does! I don't make the body fit together; you don't; your good works don't; the right programs don't; the right vision doesn't; the right marketing doesn't… God does!

Grace Isn't Finished When We Are Forgiven; Grace Carries Us to Completion

I grew up being taught that we are saved by grace. But then, somehow, I picked up that we live by merit. I have always believed God saves us, but then after salvation, I thought we must add our part to help God take us to completion. But Paul tells us grace isn't finished when we are forgiven; grace carries us on to completion. God isn't finished with you after He has forgiven you. He doesn't stop after cleansing you. He cleanses you and then He carries you. Did you catch that? He cleanses and carries. "And I am certain that God, who began the good work within you, will *continue his work until it is finally finished* (emphasis mine) on the day when Christ Jesus returns" (Philippians 1:6). Why? Because grace changes everything. "…looking unto Jesus the *author and finisher* (emphasis mine) of our faith…" (Hebrews 12:2a). God not only formulates our faith, He finishes our faith. I'll say it again, grace changes everything.

I was in a car accident when I was 17-years-old. Doctors performed my first back surgery when I was 26. The first surgery was a success, but 11 years later, I was going through my second back surgery at 37. Unfortunately, the second surgery was a bust! Only two years later, at 39 years of age, I had my third and final back surgery. I remember every stage of these surgeries in vivid detail. When I was 26, I remember lying in my bed, and to be honest, I was loathing in self-pity. I was asking all the wrong questions and making all the wrong statements. I was lying in the bed, because I couldn't walk, whining about how much my life sucked and how I deserved better. "God, I've served you. You transformed my heart at eight years old. You called me to preach when I was 13. I preached my first message when I was 14. I've been preaching for You ever since. I've been living my life for You. God, why am I in this bed in such pain when I've done so much for You?" Wow, I'm embarrassed to even write those words. How arrogant of me! However, to be honest, at the time, I didn't realize I was trying to live on my own merits. Subconsciously, I thought God owed me something. After all, I had done so much for Him.

One day, lying in bed during one of my pity parties, my loving, gracious and wise father-in-law turned me on to a book called *Transforming Grace* by Jerry Bridges. If you have never read the book, wow, you are missing an illuminating read. It will transform and expand your view of God's grace and mercy.

Grace is Getting What We Do Not Deserve

In the days ahead, as I read the book, I realized God's grace is not based on what I do, or what I don't do. It's not based on how much I serve, don't serve, give, don't give, accomplish, or fail. The definition of the word "grace" simply means "undeserved and unmerited." As I read, I began to comprehend God's grace in a new light. I began to understand grace doesn't stop when we are forgiven; grace carries us to completion. Grace cleanses and keeps me. It carries and takes me to completion. Grace is getting what we do not deserve.

After my third back surgery, more than 16 years ago, I am stronger and more flexible than I was at 17. Not because of something I did, but because the grace of God takes me from glory to glory and healing to healing. Healing was not due to something deserved. Healing came only by the grace, mercy, and goodness of God. Grace carried me, and it continued to work in and through my life. Because grace changes everything.

"He makes the whole body fit together perfectly" (Ephesians 4:16a). I realize what I'm about to say is stretching the application of this scripture beyond its original context. However, I believe these statements to be true, nonetheless. God made my back fit together perfectly. He can make your broken marriage fit together perfectly. He can make your broken relationship with your teenager fit together perfectly. He can make your broken heart fit together perfectly. He can take your bruised, beaten, and broken life and make it fit together perfectly. Why? Because His scandalous grace changes everything.

Paul states in Ephesians 4:17, "With the Lord's authority I say this: Live no longer as the Gentiles do, for *they* (emphasis mine) are hopelessly confused."

Wait, this seems to contradict with what we learned in a previous chapter. In chapter 3, we saw how God brought Jews and Gentiles together. God made them one people by adopting them into His family. But note the word "they." Who are "they"? Paul is referring to the Gentiles who do not believe. Those who are not of the family of faith. Those outside the grace of God. Paul said, "Live no longer as the Gentiles do, for *they* (emphasis mine) are hopelessly confused." He's pointing outward, to those outside the family. You will continue to see the words "they" and "their" through the verses to follow, pointing toward those outside the family of grace.

Verses 18-19 say, "Their minds are full of darkness; they wander far from the life God gives because they have closed their minds and hardened their hearts against him. They have no sense of shame. They live for lustful pleasure and eagerly practice every kind of impurity."

As you read these verses you may be thinking, "Wow, this took a dark turn. Paul had been writing about grace and unity. Then suddenly, doom and gloom." If you weren't thinking it, I was! Seems like, wow, what's going on here, Paul? Why the dark turn? But watch what Paul does. He flips it! Verse 20 says, "But that isn't what you learned about Christ." Did you see it? Paul turned it around. Remember, Paul is teaching here from the word "therefore." We covered this in chapter 4. Because of the grace, mercy, and goodness of God, therefore, this is how grace affects our lives.

Verse 21-24, "Since you have heard about Jesus and have learned the truth that comes from him, *throw off your old sinful nature* (emphasis mine) and your former way of life, which is corrupted by lust and deception. Instead, let the Spirit renew your thoughts and attitudes. Put on your new nature, created to be like God—truly righteous and holy."

Throw off your old sinful nature. Don't merely shake it off like Taylor Swift. Throw it off! If you take the time to read through the end of chapter 4 and into chapter 5, Paul gives examples of living life under the covering of grace. He explains what this new life in grace looks like. Throw off lying. Instead of lying, a person under the grace of God tells the truth. Throw off anger. Those who are under the grace of God, rather than living in anger, live in peace. Instead of stealing, they work hard and give generously. Those under the grace of God, throw off the old way of life, to put on the new way of life.

Worshiping He Over *Me*

When we live in grace, we throw off foul language, gossip and tearing people down. Instead, we encourage people with our words. We throw off bitterness, anger, and revenge. Instead, we offer forgiveness to people. We throw off the old to put on the new. We throw off promiscuity to put on purity. We throw off greed to put on generosity. It's very interesting how Paul lumps together promiscuity and greed. Because those who are sexually involved with persons to whom they are not married, are greedy. Wait, what? Paul is showing how sexual promiscuity and greed are related. Because when we indulge in sexual sin, we worship *me* over *He*. Meaning, we pursue what we want instead of what He wants.

When we live under grace, we throw off promiscuity and greed. Instead, we exercise self-control of our bodily desires and actions. We do this by walking in the grace of God. We throw off drunkenness. Instead, we live under the influence of the Holy Spirit. I love how Paul frames Ephesians 5:18: "Don't be drunk with wine, because that will ruin your life. Instead, be filled with the Holy Spirit…" Paul's intention couldn't be clearer: Don't be filled with wine; be filled with the Holy Spirit.

Throw It Off to Put It On

Paul paints this picture: "Throw it off to put it on." When I first read this, I thought maybe this was a nonchalant "taking off the old life and slipping into the new life." But I discovered that's not what Paul was saying at all. He was literally saying, throw it off! This was not a picture of reluctantly, casually, or nonchalantly taking off the old life. This wasn't, "Oh man, I really love watching porn, but I'll try to cut back a little." This wasn't, "I really like having sex with my girlfriend, but I'll ask her how she feels about it." No, Paul was showing us how a life changed through the scandalous grace of God throws off the old person, as far as they can throw it! Then, putting on the new life in Christ.

Grace Doesn't Merely Change Our Life. Grace Changes Our Whole Life Story.

We throw off the old, as far away from us as possible, to then put on the new. Paul doesn't leave you hanging and empty. He doesn't say, "Hey, throw it off. Then live your life in emptiness." So then, when we throw off the old way of life, what do we do? We put on the new way of life, so we don't stay in empty places. Why? Because grace changes everything. Grace doesn't merely change my immediate life; grace changes my whole life story, everything in my life story. Grace literally changes our whole life. This is not some reluctant trying, pushing, pressing, belabored effort, making it all about us. No, it is totally the scandalous grace of God changing everything. Paul isn't providing a punch list of actions for us to quit in our own power. He's literally pointing to the power of the grace of God.

Paul does give us a warning in Ephesians 5:6, "Don't be fooled by those who try to excuse these sins, for the anger of God will fall on all who disobey him." Here, Paul is referring to the sins he has already mentioned, such as promiscuity, idolatry, greed, and all the like. He is saying, don't be fooled by those who are trying to excuse these sins, for the anger of God will fall on those who disobey Him. Don't be fooled into participating or indulging in any of these sins. Don't participate in the sins these people promote. "For once you were full of darkness, but now you have light from the Lord. So, live as people of light!" (Ephesians 5:8).

Grace Doesn't Merely Cover Our Sin. Grace Grants Us Power Over Our Sin.

Remember what we read in Ephesians Chapter 2? Once we were dead in our sins because of our disobedience, but now because of the scandalous grace of God, we are alive in Christ. We're no longer dead in our sin. Now we live in righteousness, purity, and holiness. Why? Not because of something we do or have done, but because of the grace of God. Paul says in Ephesians 5:7-9, "Don't participate in the things these people do. For once you were full of darkness, but now you have light from the Lord. So, live as people of light! For this light within you produces only what is good and right and true." Did you see it? Grace doesn't forgive so we can walk in our flesh. Grace doesn't merely cover our sin; grace gives us power over our sin.

People often live as if grace allows them to indulge in their flesh because they have forgiveness. However, this is not the biblical function of grace. Grace doesn't forgive you so you can indulge in your flesh. Grace not only covers your sin; grace breaks the bondage of your sin. It not only provides a pardon from sin; it provides power over sin so we no longer live under sin's bondage.

Paul said in Romans 6:1-2, "Well then, should we keep on sinning so that God can show us more and more of his wonderful grace? Of course not! Since we have died to sin, how can we continue to live in it?" Grace literally changes everything in your life. Grace breaks the bondage of sin so we don't merely walk in forgiveness, we also walk in freedom. Grace provides forgiveness and freedom. Look at verse 9 again. "For this light within you *produces* (emphasis mine) only what is good and right and true." It produces. It doesn't suggest, it produces!

In case you are thinking, "Well, if I'm covered by the grace of God and He's changing my life, then He's not going to let me walk in the flesh." Wrong! Let me make this perfectly clear. Grace doesn't force. Grace doesn't manipulate. Another way to say it is, grace doesn't coerce. Grace produces. Grace produces by empowering.

What this means for us is grace changes our will, our desires, and our propensities. If I used to escape my troubles by drowning them in my drink, now I walk sober in the power of God's scandalous grace. Do you hear what I'm saying? It doesn't force or manipulate, but it does empower and produce. It changes my attitude. It changes my mindset. It changes my worship from worshiping my own desires, my own will, my own flesh, my own ideas of what I want, what I want to do, where I want to go or what I want to be. It changes my worship from worshiping *me* to worshiping *He*! Grace changes everything.

This means grace produces a change in how we view the people we meet on a daily basis. It produces a genuine love for them. We don't "love on" them, we love them. We don't love them because they are our spiritual "projects," we love them because God loves them. Therefore, grace changes how I view myself, you, them, him, and her. It changes the way we see our neighbor and the people we work with. Now people are not in my way, they are important to me and I want to take them with me on this scandalous grace journey.

Grace changes our language. It changes the way we speak of people. It changes our negative comments about other people—what they're doing, where they're not going, what they're wearing, or what they're not doing right. Grace changes everything. It changes our negativity and it gives us a positive outlook on life. It changes what we talk about, and it changes what we don't talk about. Sometimes what you don't say matters as much as what you do. Let me put it this way: Just because something comes into your head doesn't mean it has to come out of your mouth. Thinking it doesn't mean everyone on social media should have to hear it! Everyone doesn't need to hear everything you think.

Grace changes how we spend our time. Yes, grace changes everything. Grace changes our perspective on what's important. It changes our work ethic. Paul mentions how we're not working for a boss or a paycheck. We're literally working as if we're working for God. Grace even changes my attitude about work, so I don't complain all the time about being overworked or underpaid. Grace changes everything.

Grace changes what we spend our money on. Money isn't only so I can do this, or I can have that. "I earned this money so I'm spending it on myself." Bigger house, better car, more stuff to shove in the garage and forget it's there. Grace changes everything within us and around us. Suddenly, expanding God's kingdom and being extravagantly generous becomes important. Why? Because God's grace changes everything. It changes what we allow into our lives and what we do with our lives.

Grace Not Only Produces Spiritual Life. Grace Produces Life Lived by the Spirit.

Don't miss this: Grace not only produces spiritual life; grace also produces a life lived by the Spirit. We tend to think, "Well, grace gave me life, now I need to work my way to a more spiritual life." But that's not what the book of Ephesians teaches us. Paul tells us grace gives us life, but then it carries us, keeps us, and continues to work on us! So, when we look back over our lives, we can say with gratitude, "Look what *God* has done. I may not be who I will be, but I am not even close to who I once was!"

Grace grants us spiritual life, transforms our daily life, and secures our future life through the finished work of Christ. When you get down, discouraged or despondent; when life serves you lemons; when it seems everything and everyone is coming against you; when the enemy has knocked you to your knees—a perfect place to pray by the way—we have this assurance, no matter what comes our way or how hard life gets, when all is said and done, we will still be standing. In our final chapter, we will spend some time digging into the powerful, persevering power of God's scandalous grace.

Let's pray...

Father, thank You for Your scandalous grace! Thank you for breathing spiritual life into every one of Your children. Thank you for loving us enough not to leave us the way we were. Thank you for transforming us, past, present and future. When we slip into trying to work or perform our way into Your favor, remind us of Your scandalous grace that carries us to completion. Lord, change our whole life story. Give us new desires, proclivities and patterns. Apply Your scandalous grace that grants power over sin, so we will live our lives in the Spirit. Thank you, Jesus, for Your finished work. Amen.

CHAPTER 6

Still Standing

Grace assures, no matter what comes against us, after the battle ends and the dust settles, we will still be standing!

Once upon a time, long, long ago, a little six-year-old girl disobeyed her mommy. As the story was told to me, her mommy was a bit frustrated with her daughter. I've heard that names make stories more relatable, so let's call the little girl KyLe. KyLe was only six, but she had already developed quite a stubborn streak. Mommy wanted to teach KyLe a lesson, so she sternly told her daughter to sit in a chair and listen carefully. As mommy told her to sit, she took KyLe by both arms and gently helped her sit in the chair behind her. Well, KyLe was not happy with her mommy at all. So, she stood right back up. Mommy immediately said, "I told you to sit down and listen to me." As she said this, she helped KyLe sit down once again. KyLe immediately stood back up, becoming angry now and starting to cry. Mommy, gently but firmly, took KyLe by both arms, helped her sit down and said, "You are going to sit here and listen to me. Do not get up until I'm finished talking to you." With tears rolling down her cheeks and a tremble in her voice, KyLe said, "I'm sitting on the outside, but I'm standing on the inside."

Ephesians 6:10-13 says, "A final word: Be strong in the Lord and in his mighty power. Put on all of God's armor so that you will be able to stand firm against all strategies of the devil. For we are not fighting against flesh-and-blood enemies, but against evil rulers and authorities of the unseen world, against mighty powers in this dark world, and against evil spirits in the heavenly places. Therefore, put on every piece of God's armor so you will be able to resist the enemy in the time of evil. Then after the battle you will ***still be standing*** firm" (emphasis mine).

In this chapter, we will explore the persevering power of scandalous grace—grace for spiritual life, daily life, and the power to carry us into eternal life. When the world comes crashing down and circumstances are pummeling you, encouraging you to throw in the towel, quit and give up; when the enemy comes in like a flood, trying to beat you down, overwhelm and defeat you, you can rest in the amazing, scandalous grace of God. Like little KyLe, after the battle ends and the dust settles, you will still be standing!

This is the final chapter of Scandalous Grace; however, it is not the final chapter of your grace journey. Paul finishes his last exhortation to the Ephesians, and to us, with a final word. He charges us to be strong in the Lord and in His mighty power. Not your power, nor your spouse's power; not the power of your words or of your mind; no, Paul charges us to be strong in God's mighty power. Then he charges us to "put on." Remember, we looked at this phrase in chapter 5. Throwing off the old to put on the new. Now we see Paul using the same wording here as he calls us to "put on" all of God's armor so we may be able to stand against the strategies of the devil, for we are not fighting against flesh-and-blood enemies.

This is so critical for us to grasp in our current culture. Your fight is not with other people! Your fight is not with your teenager, friend, neighbor, or parents. Your fight is not with the friend who wronged you or the person who spread the rumor about you. Your fight is not with the leadership of a local church. Your fight is not with your boss or the supervisor tormenting you and making your life miserable. Therefore, what does Paul say? Put on. Throw off to put on. Therefore, because of the mighty power of God, because of the grace and goodness of God, therefore, put on every piece of God's armor so you will be able to resist the enemy in the time of evil.

Then, after the battle, you will **still be standing**! Oh, there it is. You'll still be standing firm. That should make you put this book down and run around the room for about 3½ minutes, shouting as loud as you can. Perhaps life has dealt you some hard blows. Maybe you're having a rough time: you lost your job, your spouse left you, friends abandoned you, and the battery in your car is dead. You may have heard it said, "Life is hard, then you die." This may be how you feel, but I'm writing this chapter to let you know if you are reading this book, you are still standing! You may be lying down or curled up in a fetal position while reading, but you are still standing. It's been hard, you have had battles, you have had struggles, but you are still standing. You may be beaten, bleeding, tired, worried and wounded, but you are still standing. I'll say it over and over until you get it. It doesn't matter what you've been through or what you've faced. It doesn't matter how hard or how difficult. You are still standing!

Before we look at Paul's final word, I'd like to pick up where we left off in chapter 5. You're about to see how the whole letter to the Ephesians ties together. Ephesians is a beautiful book about the Gospel story and its effect on our life story. We closed chapter 5 at Ephesians 5:18: "Don't be drunk with wine, because that will ruin your life." You may already know this, but there are some things you can do to absolutely ruin your life. Perhaps you are in the midst of self-created chaos and you need someone to show you the way out! "Don't be drunk with wine, because that will ruin your life. Instead, be filled with the Holy Spirit..." This is Paul showing us the way out! Instead of being intoxicated with alcohol or any other substance, be filled with the Holy Spirit. Instead of trying to fill your life with cheap substitutes like wine, weed, mind-altering substances or any other surrogate imitation, be filled with the Holy Spirit.

Paul continues with verses 19-20: "...singing psalms and hymns and spiritual songs among yourselves, and making music to the Lord in your hearts. And *give thanks for everything* (emphasis mine) to God the Father in the name of our Lord Jesus Christ." You read that right; "give thanks for everything." Before you take this out of context, Paul is not flippantly talking about sarcastically thanking God because you stubbed your toe. Or vengefully thanking God because the person who sped past you, cutting you off on the freeway, was pulled over and given a traffic ticket. Or thanking God because a parking spot opened close to the shopping mall entrance. Paul is talking about thanking God for everything He has done through His scandalous grace! He has forgiven you by His grace. He has granted you freedom by His grace. He is sustaining you by His grace. Give thanks for everything.

Paul continues with verse 21: "And further, *submit to one another* (emphasis mine) out of reverence for Christ." Submitting to one another is a difficult concept for some to swallow. We tend to interpret this verse as *submit or suffer the consequences!* We tend to miss the context of what Paul is addressing. This declaration represents a mirror image of the gospel! We submit to one another, out of reverence for Christ. Jesus submitted to human authorities to serve and save His people. So, we submit to each other to love, serve, encourage, and disciple one another as Christ does for His Church. We submit by comforting the hurting, soothing the broken and lifting the downcast. We submit to one another out of reverence for Christ, like Christ submitted Himself to serve those who belong to Him. Again, this is less of a mandate for people to bow down. It's a picture of people becoming more and more like Christ, through His scandalous grace. Paul then gives three examples of what submitting and serving looks like. These illustrations are often misconstrued and taken out of context, so I hope to clarify some misinformation.

In Paul's first example, he explains how we submit to one another in a marriage relationship. Look at Ephesians 5:21-22a, "And further, submit to one another out of reverence for Christ. For wives, this means submit to your husbands as to the Lord." And skipping to verse 25, Paul says, "For husbands, this means love your wives, just as Christ loved the church." You may have heard or read someone using this verse in an endeavor to control or manipulate wives. This distortion could not be further from the truth. Paul is not telling wives they must bow. Nor is he telling husbands they are to lord over their wives. It describes the conduct of married couples in their submission to each other. Are you hearing what I'm saying? Scripture is not mandating we must live this way; it is describing what a marriage looks like under the scandalous grace of God. It's not mandating what we must do; it's describing what grace produces. That's not what we were taught, right?

Verse 25 says, "For husbands, this means love your wives, just as Christ loved the church. He gave up his life for her..." Paul shows another mirror image of the gospel. He gives an example of the wife, who represents the church, and the husband, who represents Christ. So, if we're going to use this passage to manipulate women into submitting unto the lordship of their husbands, then we also must manipulate husbands into dying for their wives. Oh wait, now we're taking this too far, right? So, this is less of a demand upon couples and more an example of what a true godly marriage looks like: a reflection of Christ and His church.

Paul gives his second example in Ephesians 6:1-4: "Children, obey your parents because you belong to the Lord, for this is the right thing to do. 'Honor your father and mother.' This is the first commandment with a promise: If you honor your father and mother, 'things will go well for you, and you will have a long life on the earth.' Fathers, do not provoke your children to anger by the way you treat them. Rather, bring them up with the discipline and instruction that comes from the Lord."

If you are reading this as a teenager or have a teenager, this is not a license for parents to manipulate their children into obedience. I've encountered parents trying to threaten their children with this passage. "Obey your parents or you won't live long!" Perhaps the parents were looking for an opportunity to shorten their teenager's life. I'm not sure exactly, maybe... No, surely not. Parents would never do that.

Again, Paul is mirroring an image of Christ and His church. Because of God's grace, children honor their parents and parents do not manipulate their children. As parents and children submit to God, they submit one to the other. Then their relationships as parents and children flourish.

One of the greatest privileges and most important role as a grace-filled parent is to disciple our children. It is not the church's responsibility to disciple your children or teenagers. However, it is the church's privilege to partner with parents in discipleship.

One reason modern churches struggle is because former generations did not disciple the next generation. Consequently, we have a new generation who knows very little about God or His word. Much like scripture describes in the book of Judges 2:10-12, "After that generation died, another generation grew up who did not acknowledge the Lord or remember the mighty things he had done for Israel. The Israelites did evil in the Lord's sight and served the images of Baal. They abandoned the Lord, the God of their ancestors, who had brought them out of Egypt." The next generation did not know the Lord, nor remember what He had done because they had not been told. They had not been discipled.

So, Paul is showing an example of how grace produces submission of children and parents, which looks like the Gospel. There is a cover of grace which brings about submission and discipleship. Grace is why parents worship with their children *instead of dropping them off at church*. This is an unbiblical view of the church. The local church is not a free babysitting service. The church supports, as parents love, raise and disciple their children to be faithful Christ followers.

The third example Paul gives is probably the most controversial of the three, the relationship between slaves and masters. Ephesians 6:5-9 says, "Slaves, obey your earthly masters with deep respect and fear. Serve them sincerely as you would serve Christ. Try to please them all the time, not just when they are watching you. As slaves of Christ, do the will of God with all your heart. Work with enthusiasm, as though you were working for the Lord rather than for people. Remember that the Lord will reward each one of us for the good we do, whether we are slaves or free. Masters, treat your slaves in the same way. Don't threaten them; remember, you both have the same Master in heaven, and he has no favorites."

To be clear, Paul is not saying someone must have slaves. He's not even condoning anyone having slaves. I realize this is a hot button in our culture, so stay with me and we will learn and grow together. In Paul's culture, having slaves was common practice. In our culture, having slaves would be grounds for riots and looting. Let's see if we can clarify by shedding some light on the passage.

I would challenge you to view Paul's reference of masters and slaves through the lens of employers and employees. Let's be honest; someone employed by a company is somewhat of a slave to their employer. Yes, you get compensated, but compensation was also mandated for slaves in scripture. Paul is describing how a slave and a master treat each other when they are living in the grace of God. He's describing what graceful submission looks like. You're going to work hard to serve your employer, not because they deserve special treatment, or they have lordship over you; you submit and serve them as if you are serving the Lord himself.

You may have a terrible boss. They may seem like a slave master. Perhaps your boss is a genuine jerk. However, when we view our relationship with our employer through the lens of grace, our hearts and minds are transformed. It becomes a picture of the gospel story being lived out in everyday life. We serve our employer as if we are serving God, even when they don't deserve it. Your submission to serve may not make your employer better, but it does reflect Christ in you.

Paul does go on to describe a master being served, or for our purposes, an employer. Here is what a master/employer submitting to Christ looks like. They treat their employees with respect. They treat them right, pay them well, understanding the employee is a person, not a means to an end. The employer takes care of their employees because they are submitted to Christ and committed to help their employees succeed. Once again, this is a picture of the Gospel story, infusing and affecting all aspects of our life journey. It is literally the scandalous grace we've been talking about: the gospel story transforming every relationship and every single part of our lives. Relationships, resources, attitudes, action and language, Paul basically covers it all throughout the book of Ephesians.

The Grace of God Infuses and Affects All Aspects of Our Life Journey.

Now we're back to where this chapter started. Paul concludes this letter with a final word. He describes evil forces out to trip you up and destroy you. He paints a picture of the strategies of evil forces, rulers in high places and authorities. He talks about wicked powers and demonic spirits. As you are submitting to God and submitting to one another, there will be evil forces out to destroy everything in your life. They are out to destroy unity in the church, marriages, families, including children and their parents. He wants to destroy our unity!

The enemy's desire is to undermine unity in the Church Jesus died for. There are evil forces doing everything they can to destroy our unity—not uniformity but unity that comes through the grace of God. This is their goal. This is what they're trying to do. This is their very purpose of existence. Their goal is to destroy by causing you to compromise. They want you to compromise your life of grace. Their intent is to stand against the Church, compromise this life of grace, stop our corporate worship, destroy our love for one another and break down our submission to one another. They want us to compromise what God, through His grace, has produced in His Church.

Now Paul says, "Therefore put on..." In other words, because the enemy wants you to compromise, you must put on every piece of God's armor so you will be able to resist the enemy in the time of evil. This is what God's armor is there for. Remember the phrase from chapter 4? "Therefore, is always 'there for' a reason." *Therefore*, the armor is *there for* protection from the schemes of the enemy. Because you put on the armor, you will be able to resist the enemy in a time of evil attack. Then, after the battle, the struggle, the disappointment; after the bruises, skinned knees, and wounded heart; after someone attacked you, said something bad about you or your spouse broke their vows to you; after, after, after... After all hell has broken out against you, you will still be standing!

"Still." Give me an opportunity to focus on this word. You will *still* be standing. The only way you can *still* be standing is if you were *already* standing. You cannot fight a battle sitting down and you cannot still be standing if you weren't already standing. Now, you may be thinking I'm trying to coerce you into physically standing. Not really. I'm saying you cannot fight a battle sitting down. You cannot fight a battle lying on a couch. You cannot fight a battle in a lazy chair. You must be standing in order to engage in the battle before you. Whatever your battle, you can only engage when you are standing.

After all you have been through—and we have all experienced battles—you're still standing. Evil forces have come against you, the enemy thought he was going to kill you, but you're still standing. The enemy wanted you to give up, he had someone spread lies about you, but after the battle is over and the dust has settled, you're still standing because God grants you His scandalous grace. You may be tired, hurt, wounded, and limping like Jacob after his battle with God (Genesis 32). You might be limping, but the limp means you're still standing. You can't limp while you're sitting down. You are still standing!

Friends may leave you; your spouse may abandon you; people may say hurtful things about you. Parents may not want you; bosses may fire you; people may give up on you and walk out of your life forever. But I need you to hear this deep in your spirit: no matter what comes against you, no matter what the enemy brings your way, the scandalous grace of God will make sure you are still standing. The devil is a liar and the father of lies. He cannot defeat you when you are immersed in God's grace and armed with His armor. When God is for you, who can be against you? You're still standing because grace is holding you up. You can't trust yourself, your good works, or your good intentions. This one is difficult to swallow, but sometimes you can't even trust your own family. Sometimes your family will abandon you; but Jesus, the Father, the lover of your soul, the ever-present help in times of trouble, He is always there. He is your strength, He is your protector, He is your provider, and He is your hope. He is your Savior when you are lost, and your healer when you are broken. He will never, ever leave you. He is with you; you are still standing.

I've had people walk out of my life. I've had blood relatives who want nothing to do with me or any of my married family. But my trust is not in people. My trust is not in my resources. My trust is not in my money, job, or the American economy. My trust is not in my president nor my government. My trust is in the name of the Lord Most High who reigns in heaven and on earth. And when everything fails and falls all around me, through the scandalous grace of God, I too will still be standing!

We don't stand in our own goodness or strength, but in the grace-filled strength God places in us. We've all made mistakes and will continue to make them. I've sinned, you have sinned, we all have sinned. We all fall short, and the enemy tries to make us give up, quit and throw in the towel. He wants us to say, "It's too much, I've had enough, I can't do this anymore, I don't want to deal with this one more day."

Isaiah said, "No weapon formed against you shall prosper" (Isaiah 54:17). This tells me something discouraging and exciting at the same time. First, it tells me there will be weapons formed against us. This sucks for all involved! However, this also tells me those weapons formed against us are inferior to the power, presence, and grace of God. It tells me those inferior weapons will not prosper. The enemy can form them, he can have someone try to use them against me, but they will not conquer, and they will not destroy.

Isaiah even says, "Every tongue which rises against you in judgment You shall condemn." This tells me people are going to run their mouths against you. Someone will say something hurtful; someone will tell you you're no good, you can't make it, you're not smart enough, talented enough, strong enough or wise enough. Somebody will tell you you can't pass college or finish your education. Someone will say you can't keep a job; you won't keep employees or serve your employees well. Somebody will try to tear you down. But listen, God Himself will condemn them all. Every hater will be proven wrong because the devil is a liar, and he will not defeat you. When the dust has settled and the current battle has come to an end, you will still be standing in the wonderful, miraculous, scandalous grace of God!

Grace Assures That No Matter What Comes Against Us, When the Battle Ends and the Dust Settles, We'll Still Be Standing!

God's grace is so effective, it doesn't matter what comes against you. God's grace assures us that no matter what or who may come against us, no matter what may try to destroy us, no matter what the enemy may bring against us, after the battle is over, we will still be standing. Perhaps you think I'm beating a dead horse, but I'm going to get this down into your spirit because you've got to understand, this is all about the grace of God. He not only saves and changes you, but He also keeps and carries you. God's grace assures you will still be standing.

Paul encourages us to put on God's spiritual armor. He draws the concept of spiritual armor from Isaiah 11:5; 49:2; 59:17. He describes the belt of truth, the body armor of God's righteousness, the shoes of peace, the shield of faith, salvation as a helmet and the sword of the Spirit which is the word of God. Then in Ephesians 6:18 Paul says, "Pray in the Spirit at all times and on every occasion. Stay alert and be persistent in your prayers for all believers everywhere." It's like prayer is the glue binding everything together! Yes, we need all of God's armor; but without prayer, we are missing the whole point. Without prayer, without communication, without relationship, without intimacy, without dialog with our Savior and Keeper, we become nothing but angry warriors attempting to fight everything in sight. There are already too many self-proclaimed Christians around; we don't need one more. Therefore praying for all of God's holy people everywhere is so crucial to Paul's illustration. After all, we are not fighting against flesh and blood. We are not fighting against other people. It's very difficult, if not impossible, to fight against someone you are praying for.

Then Paul asks his readers to pray for him, too. He asks for prayer because he doesn't have the corner on the market. Paul was human just like you and me. Paul had struggles and shortcomings. Paul did what he didn't want to do and didn't do what he wanted to do (Romans 7:14-25). Paul said, "And pray for me, too. Ask God to give me the right words so I can boldly explain God's mysterious plan that the Good News is for Jews and Gentiles alike. I am in chains now, still preaching this message as God's ambassador. So, pray that I will keep on speaking boldly for him, as I should."

It's vital to note, Paul was in prison while writing about freedom. Very ironic! He was in chains while teaching about freedom in grace. Can you imagine? He understood freedom was not the lack of challenge in his life. We often feel we are not free until we are free from every challenge. But Paul experienced and lived something very different. You are free because you have been freed by grace, not because you are free from every challenge. Like Paul, you may still be in chains, yet experiencing the liberating power of God's grace. His grace is scandalous! You can be chained in prison and still be free! It would do you good to say this out loud. I know it might seem a little weird but try it; read the final paragraph out loud.

"I'm still free! The jailer can't steal my freedom because my freedom doesn't come from the jailer. My enemy can't steal my freedom because my freedom doesn't come from my enemy. The devil can't steal my freedom because my freedom comes from Christ! I may still be in chains, but I still love people. I'm still standing, still working, still worshiping, still serving, still praying, and still discipling. I'm still living and discipling as God's ambassador of His word. I will continue to put these new disciplines into practice. New disciplines exemplifying grace, unity, submission, worship, faith, and perseverance. I throw off my old life, the flesh, selfish agendas, selfish desires, anger, drunkenness, bitterness, and the like. I throw off the old to put on this new-found grace and disciplines exemplifying Christ. I will keep unity and be patient with others. I will stop tearing down people; instead, I will build them up. I will live in God's grace for me. I will not entertain evil intentions or compromise this life of grace. I will put on every piece of God's armor, and after the battle, I will still be standing! Standing with the Church. Standing, because the gospel story has transformed my life story. My story is from death to life, to perseverance, to freedom. This is the Gospel of Jesus Christ!"

Let's pray...

Father, thank You, for Your grace is good. Your grace is scandalous, and it transforms every relationship we have. Spousal relationships, kids' relationships, employee, and employer relationships, those who serve, and those who are being served. It changes everything, and the enemy does not like it. He will battle against it, but when the dust settles, Your word declares, by Your scandalous grace, we will still be standing. We love You, and we bless Your name, Amen.

CPSIA information can be obtained
at www.ICGtesting.com
Printed in the USA
LVHW040318290322
714677LV00007B/502

9 781088 012345